Everyday Women, Extraordinary Wisdom offers readers rich examples of both! This very accessible book will provide space for generous and engaging conversations in small group settings. I highly recommend its use!

—**Reverend Anne Bridgers,** St. Albans Episcopal Church

As an advocate of life-long learning, I highly recommend *Everyday Women, Extraordinary Wisdom*. The author understands and honors the skill of life-driven improvisation. This thought-provoking book reveals the value of women learning to improvise along life's journey by being active listeners and keen observers of themselves as well as others. Readers will learn how improvisation invites new knowledge, broadens perspectives, and develops new abilities, all while creating the joy of empowerment.

—**Dr. Sara E. Stevenson, PhD,** Psychologist and Executive Life Coach & OD Consultant

Everyday Women, Extraordinary Wisdom offers a deeply reflective and engaging account of how women construct meaning through their careers, vocations, and faith, weaving together themes of resilience, identity, and empowerment. Jane M. Everson skillfully elevates personal narratives to illuminate broader sociocultural dynamics. As a social work educator, I believe this book provides a rich framework for understanding the non-linear, improvisational nature of women's lives and work, while underscoring the critical role of self-trust, lifelong learning, and community in fostering individual and collective well-being.

—**Meghan Trowbridge, LMSW, LISW-AP, CBIST,** Assistant Director and Research Assistant Professor University of South Carolina School of Medicine

Everyday Women, Extraordinary Wisdom

Jane M. Everson

Everyday Women, Extraordinary Wisdom
Copyright © 2025 Jane M. Everson

All rights reserved. No part of this publication may be reproduced, distributed, or transmitted in any form or by any means, including photocopying, recording, or other electronic or mechanical methods, without the prior written permission of the publisher, except in the case of brief quotations embodied in critical reviews and certain other noncommercial uses permitted by copyright law. For permission requests, write to the publisher, addressed "Attention: Permissions Coordinator," at the address below.

ISBN: 978-1-959346-98-2 (Paperback)
Library of Congress Control Number: 2025940198
Cover Art: Missy Cleveland
Cover Design: Erin Mann
Book Design: Erin Mann

Printed in the United States of America.
First printing 2025.

Redhawk Publications
The Catawba Valley Community College Press
2550 Hwy 70 SE
Hickory, NC 28602
https://redhawkpublications.com

For Taylor Everson and Payton Dewees - two everyday women just beginning their journeys. May they be blessed with improvisational lives and extraordinary wisdom!

Contents

Chapter One: Introduction	11
The Vision	11
Improvisation	14
The Process	15
The Emergent Themes	17
Wisdom and Wit	17
The Book	17
Chapter Two: Cast of Characters	19
Beatrice	19
Beth	20
Dorothy	21
Effie	22
Janie Mac	22
Joy	23
Kate	24
Lydia	25
Moonie	26
Paula	27
Spice	27
Vicki	29
Summary	30
Chapter Three: Family and Other Childhood Influences	31
The Primary Caregiver in Our Lives	31
The Other People in Our Lives	39
Social and Cultural Expectations	48
Wisdom and Wit About Families and Other Childhood Influences	50
Chapter Four: Education, Careers, and Vocations	53
Educational Expectations	53
Experiential Expectations	55

Educational Experiences	56
Travel, Reading, Culture, and Athletic Experiences	59
Careers and Vocations	60
Career Ladders and Playgrounds	61
Finding Your Vocation	62
Wisdom and Wit About Education, Careers and Vocations	64
Chapter Five: Faith	67
Faith in Oneself	68
Faith in Concepts	69
Faith in Theological or Spiritual Belief Systems	73
Wisdom and Wit About Faith	76
Chapter Six: Marriage, Partnerships, and Children	77
Marriage and the Partnerships we Create	77
Children	79
Wisdom and Wit About Marriage, Partnerships, and Children	80
Chapter Seven: Losses, Disappointments, and Resilience	81
Grief	81
Anger	83
Forgiveness	83
Resilience	85
Wisdom and Wit About Losses, Disappointment, and Resilience	85
Chapter Eight: Summary	87
What Have I Learned from Writing This Book?	88
Lessons of Improvisational Women	90
The Interview Questions	92
Book Club Discussion Questions	94
Other Suggested Activities	95
Suggested Resources for Those Interested in Learning More	96
Acknowledgments	97
About the Cover Artist	98
About the Author	99

Chapter One

Introduction

"Tell me, what is it you plan to do with your one wild and precious life?"
-Mary Oliver

The Vision

The idea for this book took root within me in the early days of January. No surprise - January is a month when many women make lofty and well-intended New Year's resolutions. *Lose weight! Save money! Go back to school! Run a marathon! Get married! Get divorced!* I have never been one to make such resolutions. This is probably because I lack the discipline to pursue resolutions once my flute of New Year's Eve champagne has lost its fizz. However, for many years, I have made a vision board for New Year's and hung it over my desk at home.

A vision board is a collage of words and images. For me, it is an affirmation of my vision for the new year, with all the hopes and dreams as well as all the fears and challenges that a new year might offer. Each year, my vision board is a source of inspiration and motivation without the guilt that often accompanies those pesky and frequently abandoned New Year's resolutions. It is also a tool to help me remain productive during the cold, dark winter days when I spend most of my days indoors. And because life is both messy and challenging, it is also a tool to help me remember that perfection is not my goal for the year. Instead, my goal is to get out of bed (almost!) every day feeling grateful and making some contribution, no matter how small, to my family, friends, and community. That, and refraining from profanity, I have found that lalochezia is sometimes more effective than medication or meditation in reducing stress and inviting humor into my life.

My 2024 vision board included three simple, bold words: "**Write a** book." It is worth noting that 2024 was not the first year I included this affirmation on my vision board. Still, it was the first year that the bold black words seductively teased me every morning as I sat down at my desk with a cup of coffee and mindlessly scrolled through my e-mail and social media accounts. *"What am I waiting for?"* I thought to myself one morning, followed almost immediately by, *"What am I afraid of?"*

Many decades ago, I came across a book written in 1989 by Mary Catherine Bateson titled "Composing a Life." The author tells the stories of five highly accomplished women. Bateson describes how creativity and improvisational thinking shaped both their personal and professional goals every day. Bateson's bona fides are extraordinary. First, she was the daughter of the cultural anthropologist Margaret Mead, and the linguist and social scientist Gregory Bateson. Second, she was a linguist and cultural anthropologist herself and a prolific author and speaker on the changing roles of women.

Bateson's first book, *Composing a Life*, and her 2010 follow-up, *Composing a Further Life: The Age of Active Wisdom*, have intrigued me for years. I believe that many women highlighted in her books and in the hundreds of biographies, memoirs, podcasts, and TED Talks that have proliferated since Bateson's books were first published have extraordinary stories to tell. These books and other media platforms reveal impressive stories of women who took life-altering risks, faced seemingly insurmountable challenges, and undertook courageous breathtaking actions. But after digesting these books and other media, I often wondered, *"What about everyday women, women like me?"* Sometimes, all I am inspired to do is retire to my bed and consume an entire pint of Ben & Jerry's ice cream.

I began to think more deeply— *What about our stories, the everyday women busy working and raising children and grandchildren? The everyday women who are busy sustaining and savoring relationships with friends, spouses, or partners? The everyday women who are busy volunteering and caregiving for family members who are aging or disabled? The everyday women who have experienced anxiety, low self-esteem, health and medical challenges, personal loss, poverty, racism, ableism, gender discrimination, incarceration, homophobia, or other trauma and are still alive and kicking?* The *everyday women creatively improvising their lives one day at a time as they face both opportunities and challenges with grit, patience, determination, resilience, and humor? Who is allowing these women to tell their stories to a broader audience?*

As an introvert I realized that, while I might not be ready to put myself out there in a tell-all book, I could use my connections with other women to encourage them to tell their stories, and thus share with others wisdom from a few of the many women who have deeply impacted my life. I recalled one of my favorite quotes by Anais Nin, *"And the day came when the risk to remain tight in a bud was more painful than the risk it took to blossom."* I took a deep breath, and I decided to take a risk.

In mid-January, I tentatively told a good friend that I was thinking of writing a book. I reached out to another friend who works at a publishing company for her feedback on the topic I was considering. And I asked a third friend, who has been a lifelong mentor, to give me feedback on my bud of an idea. Before I could exclaim, "No! I wasn't actually going to write a book— I was just aspiring to do so in my vision board," I was committed to writing a book. I began to panic: "What in the world did I have to say?"

This book is my attempt to answer the questions I posed earlier. The women interviewed in this book are all everyday women. They haven't graced the covers of national magazines, they haven't been elected to national public offices, they haven't broken Olympic records, they haven't been the *"first woman to...."*. Or, at least, they haven't done so yet!

For this book, I am defining everyday women as typical women who are living their often messy everyday lives as friends, wives, partners, mothers, grandmothers, aunts, volunteers, entrepreneurs, employees, neighbors, advocates, caregivers, etc., without significant recognition or acclaim. Women who are facing both opportunities and challenges in their everyday lives and who, without scripts to follow, are creatively improvising strategies and solutions each and every day. As one friend summarized, *"So you want to write about women who are making up life as they go along? Isn't that just everyday life?"* My response was, "Yes, exactly! We are everyday women living everyday lives. But what we have learned - what we are still learning today <u>is</u> extraordinary and should be shared with *other everyday women."*

Improvisation

As a high school student, I considered making music therapy my career. I studied voice, piano, and percussion instruments in an attempt to develop musical technique and practice performance skills. It was then that I was first introduced to the concept of improvisation.

In music, improvisation requires a musician to adhere to prescribed musical techniques while also providing opportunities for spontaneous communication among musicians. Improvisation encourages musicians to evoke unfettered responses among each other by listening and then responding with unique melodies, harmonies, and rhythms while still conforming to stylistic elements. I remember well the musicians I met who excelled at improvisation. I marveled at the ease with which they communicated with each other, the joy they shared with each other as they listened, and the confidence they felt to explore, make mistakes, and build upon each other's offerings.

Improvisation cannot be learned in a classroom; it must be felt and experienced among musicians as they perform. They must be courageous enough to allow it to unfold without self-criticism. They must be confident enough to allow it to result in joy, even when the process of letting go is difficult. Musicians must be curious enough to allow it to offer lessons that may be applied even more creatively during their next gathering. My adolescent self lacked these characteristics; just one of the many reasons I am not a music therapist today!

Perhaps for the same reasons that Mary Catherine Bateson proposed the adoption of the concept of improvisation to describe women's lives in her writing several decades ago, I can think of no better word to use to describe the myriad ways that the lives of contemporary women unfold today. We live our everyday lives courageously, balancing family, work, and societal expectations while creatively improvising the way we communicate with each other. And as we do so, we practice, learn, and refine what we believe, what we say, and what we do. We become more comfortable and spontaneous. We begin to improvise our lives both with creativity and with joy.

We begin our lives with a structure provided by our caregivers. As we stretch our wings beyond our families, we use our experiences to develop trust in ourselves and the courage to act on our faith. We learn to embrace not only ourselves but also our families, our friends, and our communities. We learn to improvise. Life, like improvisation, is messy and full of unknowns. It is meant to be shared with joy and creativity. It is meant to be shared without aspiring for perfection or fearing failure.

Not too long ago, my young adult niece not-so-gently chided me, reminding me that I had always told her that she was extraordinary, so special that she could do anything she wanted when she grew up. However, when she reached adulthood, she came to believe that she might just be ordinary. I wish I had the words then to tell her what I know now; she is not ordinary! She is nothing less than an everyday woman creatively improvising her life as it unfolds each and every day - and that is extraordinary enough. This book is for her and for other women, young and old, who are busy creatively improvising their lives. That is, this book is for all women, like me— and you— who are making up life as we go along! May we all be more unfettered, more uninhibited, and more unrestrained even as we live and learn within the elements of our families, workplaces, and communities.

The Process

My next step after determining what I wanted to accomplish was to figure out how to accomplish it. In my pre-retirement professional life, I focused largely on qualitative research to respond to questions. So, it made sense to me to call upon these experiences and skills in writing this book. I decided to use phenomenological qualitative research techniques to gather information for this book. Don't stop reading here, please! These are just big words to justify the PhD after my name. Phenomenological simply means that I generated and asked open-ended questions of the women I interviewed in order to methodically gather and analyze descriptive information about their lived experiences, in their own words. Qualitative simply means that I used their words instead of numbers to better explore, interpret, and share their experiences with others.

I began my interviews with women who were in my circle of friends and former co-workers, and I expanded the list as these women suggested other women who might be interested in participating in the project. I attempted to reach women with varied backgrounds and experiences. Each woman was given the same list of four open-ended questions and asked to respond to them in writing or, if they preferred, in recorded interviews. (I have included the questions I used at the end of this book.) Additionally, after the initial interviews, I met with all of the women again in person and/or I spoke with them by telephone to ask additional questions. This enabled me to clarify, expand, and ensure that I fully understood their stories and responses.

Over the course of six months, I interviewed 11 women. I asked these women to dig deeply, not only to identify and describe the lived phenomena of their unique journeys but also to share the wisdom and wit they had acquired as a result of their journeys. As the introverted author of this book, I wrestled with whether to include my own story, but after considerable thought, I decided to take a risk and do so when I believed my experiences would help support or expand the stories told by others.

From the interviews, I next identified themes expressed by all or most of the women. A phenomenological qualitative approach proved to be an excellent tool for bringing these women's lives to the surface, illuminating both their similarities and their differences. While the women's stories evoked similar themes, their stories were always unique. Thus, improvisation—the act of spontaneously and creatively performing without preparation—fully describes the lives of these women. To enable each woman's story to emerge from one chapter to the next, most of the time, I used their attributed quotes. Occasionally, when a quote revealed something especially vulnerable or personal, I used it to support a theme but left it anonymous.

The Emergent Themes

Five themes emerged that were evident in every woman's story and were easily discernible. The themes, and thus the chapter titles, are *1) Family and Other Childhood Influences; 2) Education, Careers, and Vocations; 3) Marriage, Partnerships, and Children; 4) Faith; and 5) Loss, Disappointments, and Resilience.*

Wisdom and Wit

Wisdom is the ability to rely on one's experiences in order to contemplate and then act in accordance with the consequent knowledge. Wit is the ability to illustrate one's experiences and knowledge with joy and humor. As they responded to my questions, the women shared what I am calling *"wisdom and wit."* These are the culmination of the experiences that led them to become the women they are today. They believe— as do I— that these are not *"should dos or should not dos."* Instead, in the spirit of improvisation, these nuggets are opportunities to think differently, act spontaneously, laugh at yourself, learn from your experiences, relate to other people, experience joy, and develop and sustain your own voice.

The Book

Chapter Two summarizes the cast of characters who told me their stories, giving you, the reader, an opportunity to get to know these 11 women — and me— before you dig more deeply into our stories. In each of the following five chapters, I discuss the themes in more detail using the women's stories and words. And finally, in the concluding chapter, Chapter Eight, I summarize what I have learned and offer suggestions and resources for other women who may be interested in embarking on similar journeys with friends, family, and other members of their communities.

Chapter Two

Cast of Characters

"I'm grateful to be a woman. I must have done something great in another life."
- Maya Angelou

In literature and in theatre, the cast of characters is a group of people who have important roles to play in telling a story. While everyone's individual story is unique and thus interesting in its own right, it is the interplay between the characters' stories that makes a reader or audience understand their stories fully and discern how their experiences might relate to their own. So, grab a cup of coffee, a mug of tea, or a glass of wine, and meet 11 everyday women who have creatively improvised their lives - and continue to do so today. I hope you enjoy getting to know every one of these women as much as I have. As I noted in Chapter One, I have also included my story in the book whenever it felt appropriate, and so I have included my bio using my family nickname of "Janie Mac," in the cast of characters.

Beatrice

Beatrice is a vivacious woman in her 40s who has a personal and professional passion for advocacy and equity for people, especially those with disabilities. When she was a toddler, a rare cancer required the amputation of her leg and resulted in other significant medical challenges. As a young teenager, she and her family experienced the death of her older sister in an automobile accident, and a traumatic brain injury to her younger sister in a separate automobile accident. Her parents divorced shortly after Beatrice's cancer diagnosis and her mother has struggled with her losses and an alcohol addiction. Beatrice doesn't minimize the trauma that these events created for her and for her parents, but she summarizes her vocation decisively, *"I have always learned from my experiences and the experiences of others. People have to hear the truth."*

A native South Carolinian, Beatrice lives in Columbia, South Carolina with her husband and teenage son. After earning a master's degree in social work, she has been the President and CEO of Able SC (South Carolina's oldest and largest Center for Independent Living) for 15 years. There she *"elevates the disability voice"* by encouraging others to *"use [their] experiences of being discriminated against and of being treated as an 'other' to make changes."* Beatrice sees physical, attitudinal, and legislative barriers, not as immutable roadblocks, but as obstacles to be moved and removed. With her firm, articulate voice, but always with a smile and grace, she has moved and removed many obstacles already, and I have no doubt she will continue to do so in South Carolina and nationally for many years to come.

Beth

Beth is an energetic and winsome 80+ year-old woman with deep brown eyes that first engage you and a melodic voice that keeps you engaged. Beth was born in Hickory, North Carolina, the eighth of nine children. She was raised and educated in the Ridgeview community during the racially segregated 1940s and 1950s. While she recalls several instances of segregation and trauma that shaped who she is, she also recalls many positive family, church, and community experiences that have made her the joyful and engaged woman that she is today.

As an adult, Beth married the *"boy of her dreams,"* who first caught her eye when she was in the fifth grade. They began their careers and raised three children together in New Jersey. She completed her postsecondary education goal of earning a nursing degree in New Jersey and worked for many years there as a nurse and medical technician. After 37 years of marriage, her husband blindsided her with a request for a divorce on Christmas Day. Following her divorce, Beth relied heavily on her Christian faith to overcome her anger and rebuild her damaged self-esteem.

One day, as she struggled with the anger she felt following her divorce, she walked past a Peace Corps office on her way to work. As she passed the office, she recalled three recent patients who were all affiliated with the Peace Corps. On a whim, she applied and was accepted as a Peace Corps volunteer. Beth served three years in Zambia, a journey she describes as one of both *"lessons received and lessons imparted."*

After her Peace Corps service, she eventually moved back to Hickory, North Carolina where she enjoys spending time with her adult children and serving her community in a variety of volunteer roles.

Dorothy

Dorothy describes herself as a woman who is *"young, naive, and simple…always giving people the benefit of the doubt."* She chose the name to use in this book to honor a *"teacher who believed in me and taught me a lot about faith, God, and gratitude."* Dorothy was born in Hong Kong, which was still a British colony at that time, to Chinese parents. She has two older sisters and a younger brother. Chinese culture places a much higher value on sons, and Dorothy recalls without bitterness that her grandmother and mother were initially disappointed that she was the third girl born in her family. Her father was an accountant and her mother was a housewife who enjoyed playing mahjong with her female friends. Dorothy's family was not as affluent as many of her schoolmates' families were, but her father had saved enough cash when he was only in his 20s to buy the family home. Her father also invested money in stocks, allowing her family to pay the college tuition for Dorothy and her siblings.

Dorothy set high standards for herself educationally and athletically as a child and she continues to do so as an adult. As a college student, she came to the United States for a one-year exchange program where she embraced all the *"educational opportunities and resources offered to her."* Back home in Hong Kong, she applied for a visa to return to the United States to complete her undergraduate degree. While still in her twenties, Dorothy married, completed her undergraduate degree and a PhD, and gave birth to her two sons. She laughingly summarizes, *"I never had a plan. Everything just happened because I am always prepared to take on any challenge!"*

Today, Dorothy lives in a Maryland suburb of Washington, DC, with her husband and two sons. She works as an analyst for the United States government. When she is not working, she enjoys cooking, traveling, reading, and spending time with her family and friends.

Effie

Effie was born in a very small town in Alabama and has one older brother. She grew up deeply involved in the Methodist Church where weekly church attendance and youth group involvement were *"as natural as breathing."* Her parents divorced when she and her brother were very young - an event that impacted Effie and her entire family in multiple ways. She never saw her father again until she was 50 years old, when her father's struggles with dementia left him unable to even remember that he had once been married and had children.

Effie married late in life, at age 53, to a widowed prison chaplain. She credits his patience, faith, and love with helping her understand all the gifts that marriage and family could offer her. Her Christian faith, her mother's aging and death, followed soon after by her husband's death from leukemia, all continue to shape her life today.

Effie lives in Morganton, North Carolina in the home she shared with her husband and his family. After retiring from a career in higher education and non-profit administration, she founded and still directs a national non-profit that provides education and support to family caregivers of aging parents (ACAPcommunity). When she is not working, she enjoys spending time in the mountains and with friends and family, including *"my children and grandkids"* (her husband's children and their children), noting that they are the *"true unexpected joys of late-in-life marriage."*

Janie Mac

I was born in the Northern Virginia suburbs of Washington, D.C., the oldest of two children. My mother was a traditional stay-at-home mom who devoted herself to our school and extracurricular activities. My father was a career educator who often worked several additional jobs to support our family and, as a result, was frequently absent from our school and family activities. My parents struggled with their expectations of marriage; their very different childhoods in West Virginia sometimes created conflicts when they tackled financial, social, and extended family issues. As a child and still today as an adult, I often set unrealistic expectations for myself to minimize family conflict and to maintain order. I was a shy and cautious child, preferring to read by myself instead of pursuing athletic or group activities.

I chose at a young age to remain childless, but after earning a PhD in urban services I dedicated my career to education and advocacy for adolescents and young adults with disabilities. I married late in life, at age 42, and found myself living for the first time in a small city, Hickory, North Carolina. After a life of living and working in large urban areas, marriage and small-town life have been both a challenge and an adventure. Today, I spend my time writing, reading, serving on my local school board, enjoying time with my friends and husband, and advocating for my 93-year-old mother.

Joy

Joy chose an apt name for herself because she is pure joy to converse with and to be around. Just thinking of her brings a smile to the face of everyone who knows her. Having her in your life is a gift - a reminder to be grateful no matter what challenges you face, and to find joy in everything you do.

Joy was raised in New Jersey and grew up in a large and boisterous Italian Catholic family. Her grandfather and father owned a neighborhood supermarket and she loved working in the family business from kindergarten through high school. She remembers that during Easter time, her job was to weigh hundreds of pounds of jellybeans into one-pound bags. "Weighing and bagging the jelly beans was easy. The hard part was not eating any jellybeans because I gave up candy every year for Lent."

She married at age 23 and moved to New England where she and her husband raised their five children. She laughs, *"Five children under the age of seven. I was knee-deep in diapers and my life was downright wonderful!"* As her children grew and became more independent, she fulfilled one of her childhood dreams of owning her own business, a nursery school and daycare center.

As their children became teenagers, she joined her husband, a clinical psychologist, in establishing an executive development and leadership consulting business. *"My husband was a salesperson and he could easily sell executive development workshops. I designed the workshops and developed a board game and many physical team activities. Delivering the week-long workshops put my teaching skills to work."*

After a long and what Joy felt was a *"nearly perfect marriage and business relationship with her husband,"* Joy's marriage and business relationship come to an unexpected and traumatic end. In a effort to pick up the pieces of her life, Joy moved to Florida where she earned a PhD and became a university professor. Now, as she celebrates her 80th birthday, she finds herself back home in New Jersey, once again surrounded by family, the next generations of her large and boisterous Catholic family.

Kate

Kate is the youngest of three children, raised in New Iberia, Louisiana, in a conservative, religious and close-knit family. Kate was born with a serious medical condition, and as a child, she had multiple opportunities to observe her mother modeling the characteristics of a good health care advocate. Her mother's model provided Kate with these same skills and nurtured the wisdom she would use later in life as an adult advocating for her own children as well as for people with disabilities and their families.

Kate met her husband when they were seniors in high school, and they married shortly after graduation. He joined the Air Force and they lived in Mississippi and Florida before returning home to New Iberia, desiring to settle close to both of their families.

They raised two sons in Louisiana, the youngest diagnosed with Down syndrome. This news initially *"rocked my world."* However, as her two sons grew, she learned more about her youngest son's needs, *"which were both different and the same as his older brother."* She also acquired friends and mentors with similar experiences and used her mother's model to hone her own advocacy skills and become an *"agent for change."* Quietly, patiently, but forcefully, Kate guided the passage of progressive disability legislation in Louisiana, served as an elected school board member, and trained both professionals and families in advocacy skills. Kate reminds me of the proverb *"Still waters run deep."* Behind her gentle exterior, she is a force to be reckoned with as she models the way to advocate for changes in systems, services, and people.

When her husband retired, Kate, her husband, and her youngest son moved from New Iberia to Iowa to live closer to her oldest son and his family. Although surprised to find herself living in the Midwest after a life spent in the Cajun region of Louisiana, Kate has embraced the opportunities to spend time with her grandchildren, enjoy bicycling with her husband, as well as the challenges of creating a robust and reliable system of supports for her youngest son in her new midwestern home and state.

Lydia

Lydia was raised in the Northern Virginia suburbs of Washington, D.C., the oldest of two girls. Her paternal grandparents lived nearby, and Sunday dinners with them were a joyous weekly ritual. As a young child, she remembers feeling shy and having few friends: *"I was not a confident child. My greatest fears were of getting lost and being made fun of. These fears persist to some extent today."* As a child and later as a teenager, Lydia preferred to read, a habit nurtured by her mother and grandmother, rather than socializing with other children. Music was also a shared activity in her family and, along with reading, continues to be important to Lydia today.

Her parents chose not to have either daughter baptized, believing that they should make decisions on their own once they were old enough to do so. Lydia believes that this decision nurtured her lifelong exploration of various spiritual paths. Today, she practices meditation and reads the Tao daily. She credits these practices with helping her manage her lack of self-confidence and a family tendency toward depression.

Lydia married at age 30 to a man who has been a strong influence in nurturing both her knowledge of politics and public policy as well as her independence. They live in the Maryland suburbs of Washington, DC. There they raised two children, *"adults who embody many of our shared civic values, minimalist lifestyle, and stewardship of the planet."*

Recently retired, after a 40-year tour guiding career in Washington, DC, Lydia is enjoying the slower pace of retirement and hoping *"the universe will point me in the next direction life might take."* Lydia is one of the most balanced and grounded women I know; I am confident that her curiosity and delight in getting to know people and learning and experiencing new things will offer her many new opportunities in the years to come.

Moonie

Moonie is an active and athletic woman in her early 70s, although she says with a smile that she is *"falling apart physically."* A lover of animals and the outdoors, Moonie almost always has a smile on her face, and I believe that she is much more tender-hearted than she might readily admit. She is not afraid to state her opinions, however, and she is fiercely loyal to family and friends.

Born and raised in a small town in southwest Virginia, Moonie is the oldest of five children. She spent her childhood working hard in her family's tobacco fields, swimming, and enjoying the nearby mountains with her family. Moonie recognized that she was gay by the time she was 10 years old. She was raised in the Methodist church and remained with the church, even attending a Methodist-affiliated college, until she understood that the church did not support her choice of a life partner.

Following the accidental death of her mother during the summer, she graduated from college, and with support from her grandmother and other extended family members, Moonie revised her education and career goals, forging ahead while also raising her youngest sister. After a lengthy and successful career as a university professor, where she mentored many women and educators (including me), she now enjoys spending time with friends, family, her beloved wife of nearly 50 years, their companion animals, and a new passion— playing the ukulele.

Paula

Paula is the youngest of three children, raised in suburban New Jersey. She can be introspective and serious, but she is also spontaneous and open to adventure. She recalls a childhood with lots of freedom to roam the neighborhood with friends as well as opportunities to ride Greyhound buses unescorted to visit extended family in New York City and Boston. She grew up in a middle-class Levitt-style community where *"all the fathers commuted to New York City for work."* One of the distinguishing characteristics of her childhood was that hers was one of *"the only Black families in her neighborhood but, when integration came to the school system, it felt more like exposure to children from different socio-economic situations than racial integration."*

Paula has had a lifelong lust for traveling, which was instilled in her as a child by her mother. As a result, she has traveled to all seven continents and more than 50 different countries. To extend her travel passion, she even earned her pilot's license when she was in her 30s. Paula describes herself as adaptable, a trait that has enabled her to enjoy meeting people of diverse backgrounds with curiosity but without judgment, to travel independently, to embrace new personal opportunities, and to take on a variety of diverse and unusual jobs. Paula is truly improvisational, a *"go with the flow"* kind of woman in her vocational and career choices as well as in her relationships. On one of her many leisure trips, she met her future husband and landed a job as a farmer's wife in Hickory, North Carolina. She jokes, *"He married a traveler, but he doesn't like to travel!"*

Spice

Spice was born in Saigon, Vietnam, and moved to California with her parents when she was two years old. Eventually, her family moved to the Longview neighborhood of Hickory, North Carolina, where they shared a two-bedroom apartment with her aunt, uncle, and her cousins until her parents were financially able to buy their own home. She was raised as an only child in a Catholic and traditional Vietnamese household. She spoke Vietnamese with her family at home and learned English at school. Today, her father is a nail technician, and her mother is a sewing technician for a local furniture-making company in Hickory. Family is important to Spice; she is close to her parents, and she visits Vietnam with them every few years to spend time with her large extended family.

As a child, however, Spice *"despised being Vietnamese."* She recalls being embarrassed by her Vietnamese culture and language, especially as she was frequently required to translate for her parents at school events, for medical and banking appointments, when managing airline reservations, and in other community environments. As an adult, however, Spice has learned to improvise: embracing both her American self and her Vietnamese self by fitting all the pieces together like a musical score.

Spice's family places a high priority on education and food. She was expected to go to university and to excel in a profession such as medicine, engineering, or law. Her parents are not physically demonstrative. When Spice was a child, they *"demonstrated their love by putting their heart and soul into the dishes they made for me."* As an adult, Spice combined their expectations and passion with her own and earned a bachelor's and a master's degree in nutrition and public health.

Today, as a 26-year-old, Spice is following this passion by creating entrepreneurial opportunities as a personal chef while also studying and advocating for *"inclusion of food from cultures with historical significance and benefits."* She believes that *"decolonizing diets* [is important] *and recognizes that the loss of cultural food traditions has contributed to many chronic illnesses affecting people of color in the United States."*

Spice lives in Cary, North Carolina, with her partner. In her leisure time, she *"powerlifts."* Spice is an appropriate name for this young woman. She describes herself as *"neurospicy"*— a woman who embraces her ADHD label, her Vietnamese culture, her American experiences, food, and her *"overall weirdness."*

Jane M. Everson

Vicki

Vicki was born and has lived most of her life in the affluent community of Port Washington, New York, on Long Island. She is one of three children, the middle child sandwiched between an older brother and a much younger brother. Vicki is a tall, statuesque woman with an artistic flair for fashion and a quietly commanding presence. As a child, her family was active in the African Methodist Episcopal (AME) church, a small church in Port Washington founded by her great-grandfather. Her mother was also active in the community and constantly sought opportunities for Vicki to participate in the cultural activities enjoyed by the much more affluent children in Port Washington. As a result, she grew up loving literature, theatre, art, poetry, and fashion.

Vicki's parents, especially her mother, held high expectations for her to achieve as an adult in education, beauty, career, and social standing. She recalls being a quiet child who spent most afternoons after school with her maternal grandmother. As a teenager, she felt uncomfortable socially and struggled with fitting in with her peers. Consequently, she frequently succumbed to peer pressure in a quest to be *"perfect"* and a *"credit to her family and her race,"* making decisions that were not always aligned with her personal or family values.

College was difficult for Vicki. She struggled to pursue both her dream of a career in the arts and her parents' more practical dream of her becoming a lawyer. When she failed as a college student, she returned home to Long Island and spent the next decade job-hopping, becoming increasingly frustrated with the clerical and administrative jobs she found.

Even as a young adult, her belief that she needed to be perfect led her to make many egregious decisions. As a result, Vicki found herself incarcerated for three years when she was in her thirties. She summarizes her feelings about her time in prison: *"I never stood in court and asked for mercy. I accepted full responsibility for my mistakes. I wasn't angry or resentful."* Instead, she used her time in prison to teach young girls and women in the prison's adult basic education program.

When she was released from prison, she worked to create a new and different life that was more aligned with her personal values. Several individuals and programs, along with her own personal characteristics, helped her accomplish this goal. These included a New York City-based educational program for formerly incarcerated women, an AME minister and mentor, personal acknowledgment of her mistakes, her mother's support, and her reflective and insightful faith. She finished her undergraduate degree, completed a master's degree in fine arts, became an ordained elder in the AME church, helped change legislation that funds postsecondary education programs for incarcerated people, and established herself in a career as an author, speaker, activist, and mentor to girls and young women who have been incarcerated.

Today, Vicki works at Columbia University in New York as a writer in residence. In her free time, she enjoys spending time with her brothers, nieces, and nephews. Vicki is remarkably improvisational. As she creates her life each day, she continually listens to and observes the world around her, sifting through the information she receives in order to become more aware of herself and more observant of ways to communicate with and help others experience justice and build community.

Summary

The cast of characters for this book includes the 11 women whom I interviewed - and me - each of us with different characteristics, temperaments, experiences, and reflections. Now that you have been introduced to each of us, let's get to know everyone better and find out what we have in common as we share our stories more fully in chapters three - seven.

Chapter Three

Family and Other Childhood Influences

"You need a rock-solid foundation of friends and family to keep you where you need to be."
- Lily Singh

Family— no matter how it is defined, no matter if it is nearly perfect (or just appears so to those outside of the family), no matter if it is a hot mess of drama, or a bubbling cauldron of trauma and/or abuse— it shapes each of us in ways that guide us through childhood, our teenage years, and on into adulthood. Prompted by my questions, every woman began by describing her childhood experiences with her primary caregivers. Next, they described experiences with siblings, grandparents, aunts and uncles, cousins, and other extended family members. Finally, they described experiences with other adults such as teachers and camp counselors as well as memories of societal events and cultural experiences that were significant to them.

The Primary Caregivers in Our Lives

Our families of origin, specifically our parents and/or other primary caregivers, are more than just our initial caregivers. We learn from them whom we can trust— and whom we cannot trust. We learn how to express love and intimacy. We learn to self-assess our personal worth. We learn about our family's values, traditions, and the expectations that these adults hold for us. We observe— and absorb— patterns of communication and conflict management from them. We observe the way marriage and other intimate relationships operate, and we form opinions and expectations about our own future relationships. We also learn from our parents about power, money, gender roles, and relationships with other non-family children and adults.

While male relatives were important influences for some women, every woman described the women in their lives as pivotal during their childhood and teenage years. This is not surprising; historically, women have served as important role models for their daughters, granddaughters, nieces, and younger siblings. Specifically, mothers, and often grandmothers or aunts played integral roles in the lives of all the women I interviewed. In some cases, as adults, these women fully adopted the values, behaviors, and skills they witnessed and admired as children in the women who grounded their lives. In other cases, as children, they struggled to understand the values, behaviors, and expectations of the women in their lives, but once they reached adulthood they were better able to understand them and make decisions about how to fit them within their adult selves.

Lydia and her younger sister grew up in the 1970s in an affluent Virginia suburb of Washington, DC, with parents whose thrifty middle-class lifestyle made a significant impact on Lydia's life. At age 66, she is thoughtful as she summarizes her parents' influence on her lifestyle choices today as well as her parenting approach, "*My parents were not only models for thrift and careful money management, they were also models of good parenting.*"

Today, Lydia, her husband, and her adult children reside in an affluent Maryland suburb of Washington, DC, where they work hard to ignore the consumer-driven lifestyle that permeates the region. They have succeeded in making their modest home a welcoming haven for friends and family and they embrace stewardship, travel, reading, and spontaneity in their everyday lives. As testimony to her thriftiness, Lydia laughingly admitted to me once that she might still be wearing much of the same clothing she wore when she and I were college roommates!

Lydia recalls that her parents gave her and her younger sister the freedom to make individual choices in leisure activities, academic and career choices, and religious beliefs. Later, as a mother herself, Lydia extended these same freedoms to her own children, encouraging them to explore their interests in the arts, clothing choices, and dietary choices. In her career as a tour guide, Lydia encouraged those visiting Washington, DC to embrace learning about American history and to take pride in everything that traveling to the nation's capital offers visitors. Lydia embraced many of her parents' values in her own marriage and parenting roles, improvising a modern but grounded model for her own children to pursue their artistic interests.

Spice's childhood was much different than Lydia's. After emigrating from Saigon in the early 21st century, Spice lived briefly in California before relocating to North Carolina, where she and her parents lived with relatives *"until we could afford a home of our own."*

Family is very important in Vietnamese culture and Spice's family embodies this value. She describes her parents as *"the hardest working people I know,"* who are very grateful to be living in America. Today, as an adult launching her own relationships and career, Spice dreams of being able to ensure her parents' security. However, as a young girl, the only child of immigrant parents, Spice feared failing their educational and cultural expectations. She felt pressure to excel educationally and professionally.

Spice grew up speaking Vietnamese at home and English at school. She *"despised and was embarrassed"* having to translate for her parents. She recalls her mother leaning over her many times in public places, in medical offices, in school meetings *"with a big smile on her face asking, 'ong/co noi cai nhi?' meaning 'what did he or she say?' I felt like I was a 20-year old in a 10-year old's body."*

Spice describes several other instances where she was embarrassed because she believed her mother and father were submissive when faced with conflict or misunderstandings with English-speaking Americans. Her parents would remind Spice that this was *"their country,"* and Spice would retort confidently, *"No! This is our country, too. We are Americans!"*

Spice laughingly describes annual trips to Vietnam to visit extended family when she was a child. *"We would go with at least five large suitcases filled with American gifts - food, clothing, etc., and we would come back with the same suitcases filled with Vietnamese gifts."*

Although she was frequently embarrassed by her Vietnamese culture as a child, today, these experiences underpin the respect she feels for her culture, thrift, and spending time with extended family. As an adult, Spice is fiercely loyal to her family and her Vietnamese culture.

She feels tremendous pride in the many ways that food embodies one's culture and family and she has improvised a career that embraces this. Spice respects her parents' values and roles, but by the time she was an adolescent, she had learned to embrace their values while creatively expanding her own role by becoming a self-determined advocate for her own wants and needs.

Whereas Lydia and Spice describe families of origin that grounded them in thrift, family, culture, and parenting role models, not every woman describes an idyllic childhood with maternal or marriage role models that she could emulate. One woman notes, *"When I was a child, my parents did not have a happy marriage. They didn't fight or even argue much, but they never talked to each other or did anything together. My mother never had her own money. Perhaps as a result, as a child, I never dreamed of a wedding, marriage, children, etc. Instead, I dreamed of being independent in every way possible."* Another woman agrees, adding, *"Because my parents were divorced, I never observed or understood what a marriage was supposed to be. My mother was a strong, independent woman. When I married, it was really a struggle to figure out what role I was supposed to play in our marriage."* Lacking role models, both of these women learned to improvise their expectations of marriage, parenting, and family. *"Learning to partner with someone has not been easy, and I have made a lot of mistakes, but I think I am finally figuring it out!"* summarizes the first woman confidently.

Some women recall childhood experiences with mothers whose values and skills they improvised upon once they were adults. As a child in rural Louisiana, Kate experienced serious medical challenges that could have significantly impacted both her health and her adult roles as a wife and mother. Kate is soft-spoken and deeply appreciative as she describes how her mother tenaciously sought and monitored treatment for Kate's childhood medical needs. She lists these skills as *"bravery, curiosity, independence, skepticism, tenacity, and confidence."*

Later, as a mother herself, Kate was grateful to be able to practice and refine these exact skills as an advocate for her sons, especially for her youngest son, who was born with Down syndrome. Kate's ability to advocate grew as she became more confident in using these skills. Over time, her ability to improvise resulted in educational programs, personal care, and employment support for her son, due in large part to adopting her mother's skills. Only as an adult and as a mother herself, however, was Kate fully able to appreciate her mother's gifts to her. She summarizes, "*I can't overstate the impact she has had on me as a mother myself.*"

One example, when Kate was a young mother in Louisiana, illustrates her own bravery, curiosity, independence, skepticism, tenacity, and confidence. When her son aged out of an early intervention program designed specifically for young children with disabilities, professionals recommended that he transition to a pre-school program designed specifically for children with disabilities. Kate believed that her son would thrive only if he attended and was fully included in the same preschool program that her older son had attended. So, she improvised the skills she had watched her mother model in order to advocate for his inclusion in the preschool program for typical children. She was correct: her son thrived, and Kate emerged as a confident and well-respected advocate.

Like Kate, Beatrice also describes her mother as being "*a good medical advocate*" for her when she was a child and undergoing extensive medical treatments following her cancer diagnosis. However, Beatrice's observation of her mother's skills led to her creating her own advocacy model at an early age. Beatrice quickly learned the necessity and skills of having agency and being her own advocate. She frequently questioned decisions made for her and about her - a mindset she continues to follow today in her role as a professional advocate. "*When I was first given a prosthetic leg, I peed on the floor and cried,*" she recalls, laughing mischievously. "*I didn't want it or need it.*" She also recalls, with only a slight eye roll, "*being prayed over at church*" for her leg to be healed and wondering why people were praying for her when she didn't need or want her leg to be healed.

And so, whereas Kate didn't fully recognize or use her mother's model until she became the mother of a child who needed an advocate, Beatrice recognized and created a self-advocacy model for herself at a very young age. Whereas Kate fully adopted her mother's skills, Beatrice, by early adolescence understood that she must redefine her mother's skills and become her own advocate. Both women, however, learned to improvise their mothers' models in order to secure what they wanted and needed.

Effie grew up in a small Alabama town, a town where her family had resided for generations. Today, she speaks thoughtfully and frankly about the frequently stifling expectations she felt. Her mother modeled explicit expectations for adulthood that were often challenging for young Effie to understand and fulfill. She summarizes, *"Although 'Do it my way' was typically unspoken, there were times her expectation was audible. To do otherwise was a personal affront and embarrassment to her. [We] were expected to do what she wanted, without question."* Effie continues, *"There was a lot of shame in my family - failed marriages, philandering husbands, financial impoverishment."* As a result, appearance was important in Effie's family— *"clothes and personal appearance, choice of spouse and career, house and car, etc."* Understanding and challenging these expectations often resulted in tension between Effie and her mother even when as an adult, she launched her own career and marriage.

As an adult, Effie eventually came to understand that her mother was simply trying to make certain that she and her brother had the attributes she felt were necessary to being successful adults, *"making sure that we didn't fall through the cracks that so often plague children from single-parent homes. [She wanted us] to have choices that she did not have and to make decisions that she did not make."* Nevertheless, Effie struggled as a child, and still does sometimes as an adult, to overcome her self-doubts and her fear of *"not being good enough."* It was not until she reached adulthood that she was able to see beyond the family and the societal norms of her small town Alabama childhood and recognize both her mother and grandmother as strong-willed women with values and expectations that she might not fully support but that she understood and could improvise upon. In this way, Effie has been able to use her experiences to create her own model of a successful adult woman.

Like Effie, Vicki, expresses challenging expectations for adulthood from her parents, especially from her mother. Growing up as a woman of color in an affluent Long Island community where her family had deep generational roots, Vicki internalized the message early on that education was essential to her success as an adult. She understood that the *"right career, church, clothes, car, and so on"* were important and that *"not embarrassing the family or her race"* was even more critical. Vicki struggled with these expectations throughout her childhood, adolescence, and much of her early adulthood, and by her own admission, *"made many mistakes that I am ashamed of today"* in her quest to present a perfect and successful image of herself to other people.

Eventually, some of these mistakes led to Vicki's incarceration, but she feels blessed that her mother fully supported her when she was released from prison. *"The road to prison is when my mother and I first talked openly to each other,"* she recalls. Her mother was shocked when Vicki described to her the pressure she felt from her expectations. Over time, however, Vicki and her mother accepted each other's own goals and came to understand the gifts of both unconditional love and forgiveness. Like Effie, Vicki came to understand that her mother simply wanted her to have all the tools necessary to be a successful adult woman. And like Effie, Vicki has been able to use her experiences to create her own model of a successful adult woman.

Maternal expectations played a major role in Moonie's life as well, but in a different way. Moonie grew up in a large and close family with four siblings and extended family living nearby. With her lyrical southern Virginian accent, she describes her mother as an *"early feminist, someone who was interested in social justice."* As a result, she recalls that her mother made sure that their *"home was always open to any children and teenagers in the community who needed food and shelter."* Sometimes, as a teenager, Moonie found this welcoming openness very frustrating. Craving privacy and solitude, she frequently left her childhood home, moving nearby to live with her grandmother, another important woman in her life. At her grandmother's home, Moonie *"found privacy, plenty of food to eat, and support for my need for quiet and independence."*

Moonie's parents encouraged her independence while also expecting her and the older siblings to care for their younger siblings. Moonie seems to have had little difficulty juggling these conflicting expectations. For example, when Moonie was in college, she didn't think twice about helping to raise her youngest sister. *"She came to college with me when she was four years old and would stay for days, sometimes weeks, with me in my dorm. My friends and I all took turns caring for her."*

As a result of maternal expectations for both independence and family caregiving, Moonie improvised, without question, altering her own educational and career plans to assume care of her youngest sister following her mother's sudden death the summer Moonie graduated from college. Like the other women whose stories I have shared, Moonie also created her own model of a successful adult woman. She built on her mother and grandmother's expectations of independence and family support, improvising to meet her own dreams and today remains very close to her younger sister and her family.

Dorothy speaks confidently about her childhood experiences in Hong Kong. When she was first born, Dorothy was undervalued by the women in her life because she was the third girl, and Chinese culture places a high value on sons. Her mother told her that her grandmother left the hospital when she learned she was a girl, and her mother even considered having an abortion. When Dorothy and her siblings were children, her mother liked to play mahjong with other women at their apartment. As a result, their home was frequently noisy and crowded, her mother was busy, and Dorothy often had to rely on her older sisters to help her get ready for school.

Like Moonie, Dorothy frequently sought refuge outside of her parents' apartment. She spent a great deal of time at school, an environment which provided her with a quiet place for study. Also like Moonie, Dorothy learned to be independent and self-disciplined at an early age. And like the other women I interviewed, she observed her mother but then created her own model of what a mother, wife, and career professional— a successful adult woman— might look like.

When Beth was a child, her mother cared for her own children and other neighborhood children in the Ridgeview community of Hickory, North Carolina. Much like Moonie, she remembers vying for her mother's attention amongst all the children. Sometimes uncomfortable as a child with her dark skin, she smiles wistfully when she recalls being thrilled when people remarked how much she resembled her mother physically. Beth remembers her mother both as a disciplinarian and a strong advocate for Beth's educational goals. Even though both her mother and father encouraged Beth and her siblings to *"think independently, to cultivate wisdom and recognize our unique importance,"* she often grappled with self-doubt about her intelligence, her dark skin, and her goals. Only later as an adult did Beth, like Lydia, recognize that her parents held the very values and were the very role models she hoped to emulate when she became a mother herself.

Forgiveness is the conscious act of letting go of anger and resentment. It empowers us to be spontaneous and to improvise. For several women, forgiveness enabled them as adults to acknowledge their fear of failing maternal or other caregiver expectations, and ultimately to develop closer relationships with their mothers. For example, one woman summarizes, *"When I was a child, my relationship with my mother was difficult. She wasn't the mother I wanted or needed, but, as an adult I understand that she did the best she could. It took a lot of time, but forgiveness helped me see the gifts that she gave me and to be more confident of myself."*

Like all children, we internalized our mother's values, and we observed their attributes, behaviors, and skills. Some women fully adopted their mothers' models as adults and are very grateful for the skills they bequeathed to them. Others chaffed at their mother's expectations as children but recognized them as *"the gifts they were"* when they became adults. Others challenged their mothers' values and behaviors assertively as children, paving their own unique ways as adolescents. Even when we struggled with maternal expectations, however, we all relied upon the foundations our mothers, grandmothers, and other caregivers built for us enabling us to creatively improvise our own adult roles as wives, partners, mothers, volunteers, and employees.

The Other People in Our Lives

In addition to their caregivers, most women described the impact of other family members, childhood friends, teachers, camp counselors, and other adults in their lives. As we grew into adolescence, these other family members and adults helped us expand the models of adult females first offered by mothers and grandmothers. We developed relationships with other people independent of our primary caregivers. We observed these other boys, girls, women, and men and we began to express our own unique voices.

Siblings and Cousins

Siblings played important roles in the lives of most women I interviewed. As children we are thrust into relationships with these children, raised by the same caregivers. However, for each of us, our relationships with our siblings evolved in different ways shaped by our different childhood experiences and family dynamics. Lydia, for example, recalls her younger sister as a talented and confident ballet dancer and feeling awkward herself. She enrolled in a belly dancing class instead *"because it was a completely different kind of dance"* from the ballet at which her sister excelled. Both Vicki and Paula recall their siblings having clear career dreams as children and accomplishing them as adults, while they *"wandered,"* exploring several options before finding their niche.

Moonie and her siblings remain close as adults, but it is with her youngest sister that the bond is deepest, shaped in part by their mother's death and Moonie's undertaking of her role as a surrogate parent for her. As a result, the bonds between Moonie and her nieces are strong. Following family tradition, she is helping to finance their education. She smiles when she summarizes their relationship with her: *"My nieces compete with each other to have time with me. I am humbled. I am honored."*

Beatrice's world was shattered by the death of her oldest sister in an auto accident and a serious injury to her younger sister also in an auto accident. These events influenced Beatrice in ways that remain today. Personally, she is anxious about her husband's schedule when he is driving and running late. Professionally, she incorporates her understanding of family grief into her advocacy work with others.

Two women spoke of feelings of inequity and unfairness with siblings. For example, one woman summarizes, *"My family expected my brother to go to college, and my father paid for his education. While my family also expected me to go to college, if my grandparents hadn't provided money for my college tuition, I am not sure that my father would have helped me financially."* Another woman remembers her brother being complimented on his achievements by their mother, as well as by receiving frequent recognition in their hometown newspaper, whereas she received no such recognition for her accomplishments. For these women, as children and as adolescents, there was *"a huge need for affirmation and recognition"* from parents that seemed to be given more freely to their brothers. As adults, their experiences help them understand the pressure their brothers also may have felt to succeed and, as a result, they feel closer to them, including even *"feeling responsible for taking care of them."*

Beth, a woman of color, grew up in the 1930s–1950s in racially segregated North Carolina. She understood early on, from her parents and society, there were places that were *"off-limits due to our skin color."* She describes one experience with her cousins that brought this understanding fully home to her and shaped her life well into adulthood: *"When my Tennessee cousins visited my family, they wanted to go to the theatre in downtown Hickory to see 'Gone With the Wind.' There, a stark racial divide prevailed. Black patrons sat upstairs where it was dark and dirty, while white patrons enjoyed the cleaner, more pleasant downstairs area. My cousins, with their lighter skin, were directed downstairs, leaving my sister and me [to sit] in the upper section alone. I couldn't fathom why my cousins received better treatment. My sister explained it was because of their lighter skin. Filled with anger, I left without a word to my sister and walked home. I never spoke to my cousins again."* For Beth, this was an early and painful lesson that inequity and unfairness can exist both in society and in families.

Sibling and cousin experiences helped each of these women define their adult roles as parents, aunts, and grandparents. They also helped them understand, and as adults, cope better with gender roles, inequity, and trauma. Several women summarized that these experiences have encouraged them to interact now with the children in their lives in ways they perceive to be nurturing, and encouraging of independence, while also striving to be fair and equitable.

Aging Family Members

Aging family members and caregiving were significant childhood experiences for several women. Joy, for example, remembers spending time with an older aunt: *"My aunt was a tremendous example of how to live one's senior years gracefully. She lived and was active until she was 94. As I sat with her in the hours prior to her passing, she was not afraid of dying.*

I, uncomfortable with everything about dying, was crying at her bedside, but she was literally smiling, happy to be 'going home.' It was an important lesson for me."

Later as an adult and mother, Joy's childhood experience enabled her to oversee a family caregiving situation and to embrace its complex roles when one of her children underwent cancer treatment. Several years after this, Joy again used her experience to model family caregiving and a healthy respect for both life and death when she took on the role of caregiver for her ex-husband as he struggled with Parkinson's disease.

Effie's mother cared for her own mother, Effie's grandmother, for many years. Effie remembers well the time her mother spent as a caregiver and observed the dynamics between her mother and grandmother. Later, as an adult herself, she adapted the role of caregiving, caring for her own aging mother, but recognizing the importance of setting boundaries. In addition, she improvised the role once again to that of a spouse and stepmother. From observing her mother and caregiving for others, Effie understands the challenges that caregiving brings, the skills one must develop, and the boundaries one must set.

Both Joy and Effie creatively improvised caregiving models, drawing on what they had experienced as children but also adapting their roles. Joy modeled compassion for her ex-husband for her adult children and their families to observe by serving as his health care advocate. However, she also modeled balancing compassionate care with setting the boundaries necessary to care for herself. Effie took a different path. She translated her caregiving experiences into professional advocacy for others by establishing a nonprofit with national reach (ACAPcommunity) whose mission is to provide education to other caregivers. While acknowledging that family caregiving is not easy or rewarding, for both Joy and Effie, caregiving helped ground their understanding of maternal roles, marriage, family, as well as the realities of illness and death, in powerful personal and professional ways.

Childhood Friends

Friends— classmates, neighborhood children, and other children— also play significant roles in shaping children's values and perceptions.

For example, Effie, growing up in the deep South, remembers playing with all the children on the army base where she lived, including children from an African-American family. She considered these children to be her friends, but every time she came home after spending time with them, her mother would spank her as punishment for playing with them. One day, in frustration, her mother asked Effie why she continued to play with them knowing that she would be punished when she returned home. Effie, in tears, responded that she played with them *"because they were nice to me."* She continues, *"I saw them as friends. Mom only saw the color of their skin."*

In the 1960s United States, Effie's friendships with children of color were discouraged not only by her mother but by society at large. While Effie did not understand this as a child, as an adult, she understands her mother's actions, even though she disagrees with both her values and behaviors. This childhood experience helps to remind Effie today of the importance of seeing people as individuals and accepting people who are different from her without judgment. Thus, Effie has created an adult model, professionally and personally, of reaching out to people who may feel marginalized by our larger society.

Spice found it difficult growing up Vietnamese. She remembers some instances of racism and *"micro-aggressions"* from other children when she was a child in the early 2000s. *"I was called slurs by other students and peers who would make slanted eye gestures. Others would chant, 'Ching chong ling long'. As a child I didn't know that was racism and so I would laugh with them."* Today, Spice credits some of these experiences with other children with ultimately strengthening her pride in Vietnamese culture.

Similarly, Beatrice remembers some instances of bullying in school and being embarrassed in front of her peers about her physical disability. For example, she fell in the cafeteria while balancing her cane and carrying her lunch tray on the first day of middle school: *"I was covered in queso. I felt like I was going to die."* Similar to Beth, Effie, and Spice's understanding of how they fit into society, Beatrice believes that her early understanding of herself as a woman with a disability was gained in part from interactions with her peers: *"I realized early on that the world was not made for me. So, I wanted to make a difference."*

Beatrice credits her childhood and adolescent experiences at a summer camp for children with cancer for her adult values and attributes. *"I loved the director, counselors, and other campers. Not many children have to grow up as quickly as children with cancer. We experience medical procedures from surgeries, chemotherapy, radiation, needles, and countless hospital stays. We experience so much loss as our friends are dying of cancer all around us. I had to learn to cope and adapt so very early - and I wanted to comfort others."* Today, she is a self-assured wife and mother and works professionally as an advocate for people with disabilities.

Dorothy, too, recalls, *"I was not an attractive child. I had bad teeth. I had short, choppy hair. I was very tall and lanky."* As a result, like Spice, Effie, and Beatrice, she *"learned at a very young age that it is important to treat people nicely, because some people did not treat me well because of my looks."* All four of these women recognized differences and societal stigma among their peers early in their childhoods, and each chose to use the experiences to become more accepting, less judgmental, and ultimately more confident and proud of their own uniqueness.

Sometimes, even pleasurable experiences with friends can result in uncomfortable feelings that linger into adulthood. Lydia, for example, describes a frightening early childhood experience with friends that still impacts her today. *"When I was about three years old, my friends and I spent hours playing outside. I still remember the list of rules I had for outdoor play: 'Don't go round the corner, don't cross the street, don't go up the hill.' I'm not sure how I ended up [in the woods] because I was an obedient child. In any case, I was left behind by my friends. I wandered around lost for a while, but when I emerged from the woods, I knocked on the door of the first house I came to and said I was lost. They called the police, who put me in their cruiser and drove around the neighborhood until we came upon my frantic mother, who was looking for me. I don't know how much of this story is actually memory and how much I got from my parents telling me the story later, but they told me that after that incident, whenever we went anywhere, I would always ask, 'Can we find our house from here?' To this day, I have a fear of getting lost!"*

Like Lydia, I had a similar frightening childhood experience. I went to a friend's house to visit, and her mother suggested going to the community swimming pool. I had not brought a bathing suit from home, so my friend loaned me one of hers. I still recall that it was a red one-piece with a yellow badge sewn on the side. At the pool, my friend, who was an avid swimmer, jumped off the diving board several times and encouraged me to join her. I told her that I couldn't swim, but she coaxed me into jumping, telling me that swimming was easy. So, I jumped! And, of course, I floundered for what felt like forever. I was rescued by one of the lifeguards who was furious with me because the yellow patch on my bathing suit meant that the child wearing it had passed the swimming test necessary to be in the pool. Like Lydia, my experience still impacts me today. I still can't swim comfortably and, as a result, I won't go in a canoe, kayak, or pool without serious life jacket protection. (A few years ago, I was talked into white water rafting with my family at the US Whitewater Park. I was enjoying the experience until someone from our raft fell in the water, and I realized that if I fell in, I would need to swim back to the raft. That was the end of my white-water rafting enjoyment!)

For many of the women, seemingly simple childhood interactions with friends, as well as more intensive interactions with friends, remained significant into adulthood. Whether we have remained friends seems less important than the experiences we shared with them. For Dorothy, one experience shaped her fears as well as her values: *"When I was about 14 years old, one of my classmates died from cancer. When she first became ill, I asked her how she was doing, and she replied, 'Well, for once I would like to make it to church on time!' I thought that was an interesting response; I didn't know what to make of it! Her death later had a huge impact on me. It made me realize that I don't want to live with regrets. If I want to do something, I will do it!"*

Childhood interactions with others can damage or build self-confidence, reinforce shyness or extroversion, encourage kindness or bullying, clarify values, and/or diminish or expand our understanding of diversity. What we remember shapes us as we struggle to make these experiences a part of our whole self. One woman summarizes what many women expressed in their stories: *"As adults, we must remember our own childhood fears and other traumatic experiences. This helps us learn about ourselves and how and why we react in the ways we do. It also helps us be sensitive to the children in our lives and their experiences. Listening to their stories helps them react to their experiences even if they feel insignificant to us."*

Teachers and Other Adults

Other adults, besides our parents and other primary caregivers, also help shape our values and perceptions. Teachers especially play a significant role in the lives of children and adolescents. Most women I interviewed recall positive experiences with *"teachers who made a difference by taking the time to listen, to ask questions, and to dedicate extra time to individualized instruction."* Dorothy, for example, remembers a teacher who believed in her abilities and taught her *"a great deal about faith, God, and gratitude."* Beatrice recognizes the impact that enlightened doctors and nurses had on her during her frequent hospital stays for cancer treatments, *"allowing me to have typical childhood experiences even while hospitalized."* As for me, I was a Girl Scout from Brownies through high school. I remember, when I was in high school, I idolized a college student who was my troop leader— an experience that encouraged me to volunteer as a Girl Scout leader for several years when I was in college.

But teachers and other adults may also destroy a child's faith in them. Beth shared a story that illustrates this: *"In my senior year of high school, a male teacher touched me inappropriately. I kept silent even when my parents questioned me about why I wanted to quit school. As a young person, I failed to recognize the severity of an adult teacher's actions. I never told my mother or sought help even when he deliberately assigned me low marks to ensure my silence. My idealistic view of teachers as mentors was shattered."* As an adult, Beth recognizes that coming forward to confront abuse from an adult requires confidence and courage, skills that many children won't develop until later in life. She hopes that sharing her story encourages other children and young women to recognize inappropriate behaviors from adults and to reach out to parents or other trusted adults as soon as they feel uncomfortable.

Societal and Cultural Influences

Societal experiences and influences also shaped the lives of the women I interviewed. There is no doubt that children today are heavily influenced by social media, technology, environmental change, and other seismic political and cultural changes. Whether today's influences are greater than those experienced by the women I interviewed is a subject for a different discussion, but there can be no disagreement that these 11 women and I were all impacted by societal experiences and cultural influences during our childhoods. As children we experienced the impact of wars, political upheaval and assassinations, racial riots, space exploration and disasters, and much more. As children, without a score to follow, we improvised our reactions by observing those around us, and only now as adults are we able to reflect on how these events shaped our lives.

Discrimination and Inequity

The impact of societal and systemic discrimination and inequity, specifically on Beatrice, Beth, Effie, Paula, Vicki, and Spice's young lives, was life-altering. Each grew to understand that skin color, ethnicity, disability labels, and social class all mattered far beyond their own families and communities, but they also grew to understand the importance of *"becoming comfortable in your own skin."* They learned the importance of getting to know people, being curious instead of judgmental about differences, and accepting people as individuals with their own unique experiences and expectations. As children, they lived within the norms of their families and their childhood communities, but they also used their experiences to create positive opportunities for themselves. Beth, now in her 80s, summarizes her adult philosophy of gratitude and forgiveness: "*It was hard won, but now more easily lived: With goodness and love, I perpetually seek rainbows above.*" A much younger Spice notes, "*I am still working on breaking stereotypes and stigma.*" Beatrice reflects on her role as a professional mentor to others: "*I encourage my staff to use* [their] *own experiences of being discriminated against, being treated as an 'other,' to make change.*"

Paula's experiences growing up in New Jersey in the 1960s were very different from Beth and Effie's experiences growing up in the southern United States, but they were no less influential. "*When I started grade school in 1966-1967, I was one of very few non-white students. That all changed in third and fourth grade. Kids, predominately Black and Hispanic, were bussed to the elementary school I had attended since kindergarten. Seeing Black kids was not novel to me since we were very connected with my extended family in Boston and New York City. For me, integration meant white kids were getting exposed to Black kids and Black culture. And while the Black kids weren't novel to me, their economic status was. We were a middle-class family. The bussed kids typically were not. They got free lunches and you could tell their families struggled. Mine did not."*

Beth's experience as an adolescent traveling by train from North Carolina to New Jersey to visit family was another poignant lesson in the complexities of racial inequality. *"Upon the train's arrival in Washington, DC, my nine-year-old nephew and I disembarked to change trains. He urgently needed to use the bathroom. To my dismay, we were directed to the segregated 'colored' bathroom, which happened to be far away from our location. We were in the capital of the United States, but we were looked upon as if we didn't matter. At that moment, I vowed never to sing 'America the Beautiful' or pledge allegiance to the American flag again. To this day, I don't do either. Inequality leaves me both angry and sad."* Beth's recollection both saddened and inspired me. Her memory is harsh, and her reaction a reminder of what far too many people feel about aspects of the United States. However, I also find her to be a courageous and resilient woman who has used this (and many other) experiences to grow into a woman with strong family ties and community leadership experiences.

Similarly, Spice recalls an experience with her mother while waiting in line at a major airport. *"We were standing behind a mother and her daughter. I was about nine or ten years old. We didn't see the 'Wait Here' sign, and I guess we were standing too close to them. The woman turned around, waved her hand, and shooed us away. Then she clutched her purse to her chest and moved her luggage close to her as if we were going to steal something. I was filled with rage. At first, I thought it was my fault, but then I realized it was racism. That was my first experience with racism."*

Social and Cultural Expectations

Effie grew up in an Alabama family that was *"poor as church mice,"* but her deeply southern family displayed their silver, cut glass, and china proudly and defiantly, a statement of *"what was true in previous years and generations, even though it belied our current reality."* In addition, during Effie's childhood, divorce carried a stigma that, thankfully, is lessened today. Effie recalls with deep shame a classmate telling her that she couldn't play with her because *"her mother was not a nice lady"* because she was divorced. Similarly, Vicki recalls family expectations of *"perfection"* and notes that *"a lot was expected of me because* [my family] *saw great possibilities in me. Whatever came down from the ancestors was expected."* For Effie in Alabama and Vicki in New York, but for different reasons, they learned that the image one presented to the world outside of the family was perceived to be of the utmost importance.

Growing up in the New Jersey suburbs of New York City during the 1960s, Paula remembers, among other things, the assassination of Martin Luther King and the riots that followed. She remembers the positive impact of meeting Shirley Chisholm (the first Black woman to be elected to the US Congress) during a visit to her hometown. Later, living in Washington, DC, she recalls the early days of affirmative action and wondering whether people felt she was accepted to Georgetown University because of the color of her skin. These events helped her to develop a deeper sense of her self-worth and her independence.

In my own adolescence, I remember attending one of the first Earth Day events in Washington, D.C., in 1972 and being concerned by the messages I heard about overpopulation and climate change. The event was pivotal for me. I chose vegetarianism and voluntary childlessness, two decisions that have shaped my life philosophically, financially, and socially for the past 50 years. The experience deepened my lifelong interest in healthy eating and my connections to my extended family.

All of the women I interviewed realize that our expectations and experiences from childhood shaped the values we hold dear today and how we view the world. Many were positive influences, clarifying our values, strengthening our resolve, honing our discipline, and helping us set goals. Other influences caused us to struggle with making sense of injustice, racism, sexual abuse, ableism, and other complex issues. As adults, we look back on these experiences, sometimes with anger and disbelief, sometimes with humor and embarrassment, but ultimately with both wisdom and wit.

Wisdom and Wit About Families and Other Childhood Influences

• *"I think you have to be an adult— perhaps even a parent yourself— before you can truly understand your own parents. As children, we often see them as 'good' or 'bad,' but that way of thinking is too simple. Parents are flawed humans— just like we all are— most of them do their best while trying to figure out how to raise healthy, happy children. Don't waste your time being angry with them. Forgive them and learn from them."*
• *I imposed perfectionism on myself. Don't be afraid to fail. Don't fear not being as good as others. Don't feel like you must be a role model for other women."*
• *"Learn to be clear about your own personal values - know what you will and will not stand for."*
• *"I wish all women would have the opportunity to experience the kind of guidance I received from family members, friends, and mentors throughout my life. I have no doubt that without the knowledge, patience, and support I received, I would have been daunted by the challenges I have faced, and I would have missed opportunities for learning and personal growth."*
• *"Teachers, ministers, scout leaders, and other adults offer children and adolescents opportunities to learn about adult roles outside of their family. When they use their power to betray a child's trust, it is devastating and can be a life-long source of anger and shame. Please listen to children and encourage them not to be afraid to speak up and seek guidance from a trusted adult."*
• *"Everyone needs a community. Building communities of support in one's personal life is what sustains individuals and families."*
• *"It is important for adults not to underestimate the impact that current events can have on a child. It is okay to tell them, 'I don't know why this is happening' or 'I am frightened and sad, too.' It is not okay to try to hide the news from them or to pretend that it won't impact them. Talk to them— you don't need to have the answers, you just have to make the time to listen."*
• *"Dream! Set goals! Envision yourself in the future! Consider yourself at age 90, looking back on your life. Put in place now those pieces that you think you*

Jane M. Everson

will wish later had been part of your life."
• *Laugh at your younger self! Forgive yourself for your foolish deeds. Forgive others for their foolish deeds."*

Chapter Four

Education, Careers, and Vocations

"The education and empowerment of women throughout the world cannot fail to result in a more caring, tolerant, just and peaceful life for all."
-Aung San Suu Kyi

Education is a shared value among all the women I interviewed. Every woman, without exception, noted that her family placed a value on formal education, including an expectation to excel in elementary school through high school, and frequently an expectation to graduate from college or pursue graduate education. Rarely, however, was the expectation solely for the sake of learning. Instead, most women felt pressure to excel for a myriad of reasons— to marry well or be financially independent of a husband or partner, to be a credit to their race or ethnicity, to make the most of American resources and opportunities, and/or to make their families proud.

Experiential education, including travel, reading, athletics and sports, music, arts, and other cultural events, was also an important value. Many women fondly remember school or community centers, summer camps, church youth groups, Girl Scouts, and time with their families and/or with friends as vehicles for providing these opportunities. As a result, most women continue to relish these opportunities as adults, joining book clubs, playing tennis or pickleball, revisiting musical instruments they enjoyed as children, and/or traveling to countries where they or their ancestors previously visited or resided.

Educational Expectations

Effie summarized her mother's educational expectations: *"You go to kindergarten. You go to elementary school. You go to high school. You go to college. Then we can talk about you stopping your education."* Spice concurs with Effie, summarizing her Vietnamese parents' reaction when she suggested to them that she might not go to college: *"You are our only child. We made it this far. You are going to college."* Kate, Vicki, Paula, and I also agree that our families had comparable expectations for education and that success was expected. Lydia remembers, *"My parents always expected me to do my best. I don't remember ever being punished. To me, the worst punishment was one of them saying, 'I'm disappointed in you.'"* Paula notes, *"I was a B/C student when I didn't care. I was an A/B student when I was motivated by fear of my mom."* Vicki agrees, *"I was afraid of my mother's anger if I failed."* Kate, who was uninterested in completing college and pursuing a career, recalls her family's support when she dropped out of college: *"I dropped out of college after one semester. I missed [my future husband] who had remained in New Iberia, Louisiana. My parents were disappointed but accepted my decision. This was an example of the unconditional love my brothers and I always received from our parents. Even when we chose different beliefs or made decisions that disappointed them, they still supported and encouraged us."*

Dorothy recalls her Chinese father's unmet educational dreams and sage advice: *"He was so poor, but he invested money to pay for our educations. He had a lot of unfulfilled dreams; he thought education was so important because he suffered during [World War II] and could not finish his education because of the war and his health. He said, 'I can leave you all the money in the world, but someone can take it away from you. No one can take your education away from you.' I listened and I studied."*

Likewise, Moonie summarizes the value her family placed on education. One of her most powerful childhood memories illustrates her rural Virginia family's respect for work and education. *"My grandparents assigned each child a few acres of land and required us to raise tobacco from the beginning to the end— from planting to market. We were allowed to keep any profit we made as long as we used it for education."*

Several women noted that specific vocational guidance was limited from their families and high school guidance counselors. I recall being advised in high school that education, nursing, and social work were *"appropriate careers"* for women. I also recall that one of my strongest elementary school memories is of our 6th-grade yearbook with class predictions for our adult lives. Mine said, *"Janie, with many a fine feature, will one day be a good teacher."* And so, I did! Similarly, Beth's dream was to become a nurse, and Joy's goal was to be an elementary education teacher. Many women remember goals of *"going to college and finding a job* [they] *loved,"* but struggling to identify career goals. *"I was not the kid who had career goals figured by the age of three. My hopes were to finish college. My fears were that I wasn't smart enough,"* recalls Paula. Several women recall that their parents valued education not just for career preparation but also as preparation for *"good"* marriages or for *"performing in the world."*

Broad family and societal expectations for completing formal education with somewhat limited career expectations were likely a characteristic of the 1950s -1970s, during which most of these women completed high school, attended college, and contemplated next steps. In some instances, these broad expectations may have enabled their creative career improvisation— jobs as a tour guide, bartender, paralegal, travel agent, pollster, casting director, art festival producer, conference planner, non-profit founder, and prison ministry. For other women, however, the parental expectation was very clear: pursue a professional degree and a career in medicine, engineering, business, or law. Lydia, Vicki, and Paula all remember feeling *"less supported"* to pursue studies in airline pilot training programs, liberal arts, or the fine arts, even when their interests and talents flowed in these directions. I, too, remember being dissuaded by male faculty from pursuing my interest in veterinarian medicine during my first year at university. On the other hand, Spice, the youngest of the women I interviewed, is an example of a creative and improvisational woman of the 2010s. Even when she felt pressure from her parents to pursue a professional career, she instead wedded her passion for food and health with her entrepreneurial spirit and became a personal chef and advocate for the expansion of healthy cultural food opportunities.

Experiential Expectations

Several women recall their families holding specific values not only for formal education but also for experiential opportunities. Moonie,

Paula, and Joy, for example, all recognize their family's belief that travel is an essential component of education, and they still value travel as adults. Almost every woman underscored the importance of leisure reading in their families and, as a result, have grown up loving to read as adults, *"both as a means of escape and as a means of learning."* Music, arts, cultural, and athletic experiences were important in several women's families, including my own, and remain important to us as adults.

Educational expectations for all of us were motivated by a variety of family values and childhood experiences as well as by societal expectations. We recall a balance of formal and informal educational experiences, the combination of which has provided us with knowledge, values, attributes, and dreams that we still nurture today. Our experiences— the paths that brought us to adulthood, however— are unique and improvisational.

Educational Experiences

Beth recalls her high school experiences at Ridgeview High School in North Carolina, especially her junior and senior years, as *"a path marked with significant events."* She describes her feelings about a title she ultimately won. *"During my junior year, I wanted to be a Debutante Queen, but one committee member seemed intent on excluding me. Her criteria were prettiness, fair skin, and intelligence. I grappled with self-doubt, largely influenced by my dark skin. Despite the hurdles, I eventually claimed the title. My dreams appeared elusive, yet I resolved not to yield to the high school pressures that weighed on me. I fiercely guarded my aspirations."* After high school, Beth's determination and her parents' belief in her enabled her to achieve her dream of earning a nursing degree.

Paula and her family had moved from New Jersey to Washington, DC, when it was time for her to enroll in college. Her father worked at Georgetown University, and when she was accepted, she was excited even though she wondered if people assumed her acceptance was the result of affirmative action. Paula didn't have specific career goals. *"At some point, I wanted to be a Supreme Court judge,"* she laughingly recalls, *"because I heard they were the ultimate rule makers."* She struggled for her first two years, fearing that she wasn't smart enough and recognizing that she lacked some critical study skills that her classmates had acquired in their high school prep programs. With help from classmates, Paula summarizes, "I went from a struggling freshman to a powerhouse in my junior and senior years. I ended up as an English Lit major because an advisor told me, 'If you can write, you can think.' That made sense to me."

Effie graduated from Berry College in Georgia, a school founded by a woman and heavily rooted in non-sectarian Christian values. In college, Effie continued to struggle with childhood feelings of self-worth and shame but found that the college motto, "Not to be ministered unto, but to minister," aligned well with her personal goal to have a career making a difference. "The college culture and my experiences and mentors led me to graduate school and a 20+ year career in higher education student services, non-profit management, and prison ministry."

Dorothy embraced all the educational opportunities available to her in her Catholic kindergarten through high school program in Hong Kong. "I feel fortunate for those educational opportunities. I tested into the school— it was a good school. I learned there that I have good math abilities." Dorothy learned early to be independent and to rely on herself to pursue her academic goals. "Making it to school was a challenge. I had to iron my own uniform, but my oldest sister was a big help. My mother did not think that she needed to help me. She did not have a mother when she was a child so she felt I should be able to take care of myself. By the time I was in first grade, I was on my own— my sister was five years older, and she had moved on."

By high school, Dorothy had developed a regimented and busy schedule and had set firm educational goals for herself: "I got to school early, and I spent time there doing my homework in the mornings. I developed good study skills in the hours I spent at school by myself. My ability to do well as an adult, I attribute to education. My job was to study." Dorothy's drive enabled her to complete college and graduate degrees, earning a PhD by the time she was 30 while balancing work, marriage, and children.

Dorothy recalls several positive mentors in college and graduate school who helped her, especially when she was juggling marriage, family, school, and work. But Dorothy also remembers an experience in graduate school that taught her the importance of standing up for oneself. "*I received a [National Science Foundation] grant, which provided a cash award for the student, but the thesis advisor was the actual grant recipient. The thesis advisor kept me in school for an additional year as a student so that the research credit would be in her name as a faculty member. I had lots of well-meaning mentors until then— this was a good lesson for me that not everyone was there to help me.*"

One of Joy's proudest accomplishments was earning her PhD at age 70 and embarking on a third career as a university professor. She describes her experiences, "*I loved the opportunity to share my experiences and knowledge and my personal life with students who were preparing to enter the job market. I taught communication skills and personal development. Ten years later, I still hear from my students.*"

As for me, I enrolled at the University of Virginia (UVA) in one of the early classes of women to be fully admitted as undergraduates. This followed a contentious legal battle to require the state's flagship university to become coed, a battle that was still being fought by some faculty and male students in 1976 when I enrolled. I was academically prepared, but I was immature and naive socially. I recall taking a circuitous route to classes every morning so that I wouldn't have to pass a stone wall where male students sat holding signs numbered 1-10 to rate the women who walked by. At age 18, it never occurred to me to be angry or to complain to university administrators.

Lydia also enrolled at UVA, and we met as second-year students. Like me, she lacked self-confidence. She recalls making a conscious decision when she entered university: "*No one at UVA knew me as the shy, nerdy, bookish, and insecure person I was in high school. If I could fake being outgoing and confident for long enough, people would begin to see me as that person. And it worked! I don't think anyone from that time period has any idea how often I felt— and still feel— insecure about whether people like me.*"

One experience at UVA was pivotal for me. Along with several other young women, Lydia and I founded the university's chapter of a national sorority. From a fledgling group of a dozen women or so (mostly women like us, who were shy and awkward, not what we considered to be typical sorority girls), the sorority grew to about 50 young women. In our last year of university during our final rush activity, we invited and rushed a young woman of color. When the votes were tallied to offer a bid to her, two women voted *"no."* Chaos ensued—arguing, accusatory comments, people resigning, and ultimately, one woman called the campus newspaper to report what had happened.

Instead of resigning from the sorority as several of our friends did, Lydia and I decided to remain and attempt to change the culture from within. Today, both of us question whether the better decision would have been to resign, but for me, the decision to remain impacted me both professionally and personally. After graduation, over the next 40 years of my career, I found myself employed in, or consulting with, dozens of organizations that were fundamentally sound but needed leadership and cultural change. I believe that my sorority experience prepared me well to listen, observe, encourage diverse perspectives, establish vision, and advocate for the hard work necessary for organizational and cultural change. As I finalize this book today, at the beginning of 2025, I also realize that I must draw on this same wisdom to address issues important to me in our current American political environment. I will not abandon America because I believe that it is still a fundamentally good country that needs hard work from its citizens to live up to its vision.

Travel, Reading, Arts and Culture, and Athletic Experiences

For several women, travel experiences have been life-altering. Travel *"opened my eyes to the ways other people lived, allowed me to experience the feeling of being where my family came from years and years before"* and *"changed the way I looked at news or read an article in the newspaper,"* summarizes Joy. Paula appreciates her mother's influence on her lifelong passion for traveling: *"My mom's love of traveling was planted in me honestly. Her hobby became my bad obsession!"* As an adult and mother, Lydia has enjoyed many family vacations, sometimes surprise trips planned by her husband as ways of learning and experiencing new places and cultures. And of course, her job as a tour guide in Washington, DC, enabled her to share history and culture— two of the primary gifts of travel— with thousands of American students and adults.

For several women, and for me, reading for pleasure was initially a way of coping with childhood and adolescent shyness and lack of self-esteem. As adults, however, these pursuits have remained important to us as ways of growing, experiencing, and learning. *"Today, I still read for enjoyment and to escape the cares of the day. Books help me connect events in history and to learn more about places, culture, and lifestyles that are unfamiliar to me,"* summarizes Lydia. Vicki concurs assertively, *"I am an avid reader. I have a love of words."*

Vicki recalls her mother seeking out multiple childhood opportunities for her to study art and music— a passion she retains today. Both Lydia and Moonie describe music as an important way of sharing family time together as children— again, a passion that remains with them today. I was fortunate to have grown up in the shadow of Washington, D.C., a city that provided ample opportunities for school trips to the Smithsonian Museum, the White House, the Capitol, and the Supreme Court. I believe these childhood and adolescent experiences strongly influenced my interest in politics and community engagement today.

Both Moonie and Dorothy were athletic as children and credit this with teaching them discipline and self-confidence. Joy and Kate also remain physically active as adults, and along with Effie and Lydia, describe many family activities centered around boating, hiking, bicycling, playing tennis, etc. Although I didn't recognize at the time that the passage of Title IX of the Education Amendment Acts of 1972 had opened athletics to girls and women, I remember a sudden burst of offerings to girls in my junior high and high school. I attempted basketball, field hockey, bowling, golf, volleyball, and tennis— unfortunately, all sports at which my physically uncoordinated adolescent self definitely did not excel!

Education shaped the lives of every woman I interviewed, offering not only vocational and career skills but also life lessons in community service, leadership, and balancing life's responsibilities.

Careers and Vocations

A job is a paid position that provides a woman with the financial resources to make a living independently or to contribute financially to a marriage, partnership, and/or family. A career, on the other hand, encompasses one's overall work history, generally a sequence of jobs or positions over many years or throughout one's life.

A vocation describes a calling to do work that gives meaning to one's life. A vocation may be one's paid work, or it may be work that is outside of one's wage-earning activities. For example, some women find marriage, raising children, spending time with grandchildren, or doing volunteer work to be their vocation. Other women find artistic pursuits, spending time in nature, or gardening to be their vocation. Still, other women find their vocation through a religious calling, either to some type of ministry or to volunteer work within their chosen religious tradition.

A woman may (or may not) feel that her job or career is a vocation. Among the women I interviewed, several women, especially when they first entered the work world, described floundering in paid positions that did not ignite their passions. They often struggled until they found their way, either through different paid jobs or through outlets other than paid work. Still, other women were able to combine their callings with paid jobs early in their lives and build life-long careers that addressed their passions.

Career Ladders and Playgrounds

Every woman chose to pursue a unique path as she built her career. Some women climbed the traditional career ladder. They completed educational requirements and applied for jobs that would take them from step one to step two, three, and so on up a career ladder. Dorothy, Moonie, and I followed traditional career ladders— completing educational credentials, securing positions with ever-increasing opportunities for academic research, writing, and teaching. Similarly, Beatrice completed her academic credentials, worked a few jobs to gain experience, and then found her career as President and CEO of an Independent Living Center. These women and I had specific education and career goals in mind as young women; we pursued all available opportunities to accomplish our goals.

Other women *"bounced around in a playground of paid jobs"* throughout their lives, *"swinging from one job to another, sometimes falling off the monkey bars,"* but bravely climbing back on with new and sometimes unusual jobs. Often, these women accepted jobs that required novel skills from their previous jobs. They were truly improvisational, courageously embracing new opportunities and learning skills and earning credentials as they worked. Throughout her career, for example, Paula improvised a degree in English literature into a variety of diverse careers, including working as an arts festival organizer, a casting director, in student services within higher education, in tourism, and most recently, in publishing. Lydia, an English and Communications major, also improvised her degree into a successful career in tour guiding. Similarly, Joy translated her degree in education and her skills as an educator into a career as a professional trainer and coach in corporate America. Kate also improvised creatively and confidently, using her *"lived educational experiences"* as a mother and disability advocate, to teach a morning pre-school class, to serve as an elected school board member, and to work with professionals and other families as a trainer in student instruction, team building, and family engagement.

Some women reached their goals and then stepped back and set new goals. Sometimes, career improvisation occurs later in life when women realize that their jobs either never met their dreams or no longer meet their dreams. For others, it occurs when they are more financially secure and/or when caregiving and other family responsibilities are no longer pressing. For example, Effie retired from a career in higher education and non-profit management to establish her own non-profit that met a need for caregiver education and support that she identified from her own caregiving experiences. Likewise, Vicki relied on her experiences as an incarcerated woman to establish a career in advocacy, writing, and public speaking for other incarcerated people. Beth found her calling after her divorce, using her faith to help her determine her next steps as a Peace Corps volunteer.

Finding Your Vocation

Whatever path they chose, I think all the women interviewed would agree that it is important to create a fulfilling life, *"a life that is not just about getting through the day."* The word vocation derives from the Latin word *"vocare,"* meaning *"to call."* A vocation, whether secular or religious, comes after a long process of experiences and discernment. It begins in childhood with people asking you, *"What do you want to be when you grow up?"* It continues through adolescence and adulthood as we learn to trust ourselves, articulate our personal values, dissect our experiences, and embrace paid and volunteer work experiences.

No matter what paths they thought they were following, these women ultimately followed unknown paths that included detours and obstacles created by death, divorce, incarceration, illness, children, family caregiving, and other experiences. For example, being in the right place at the right time, *"waiting at a bus stop"* enabled Paula to learn about a graduate program that would enhance her career and lead to her vocation in the travel industry. For Vicki, time spent in prison gave her time not only to reflect on her values, but also to deepen relationships with people and organizations that would ultimately help her fully define and pursue her vocation. For Joy, divorce gave her the flexibility to move to a different state, complete her doctorate, and pursue a new career without her ex-husband and former business partner. For Beth, divorce gifted her the anger she ultimately needed to find her vocation as a Peace Corps volunteer and community leader. For Beatrice, her cancer diagnosis set her on a path to pursue advocacy and equity for other people with disabilities. For Kate, her own medical needs and the needs of her son with Down syndrome gave her the skills and experience to become a leading advocate for other families with children with special needs.

Perhaps in no other area of life does improvisation play a greater role than in one's career and vocation. We must trust ourselves to make decisions about what to do, when to do it, and where to do it. We must allow our work to evolve without self-criticism. We must take steps to ensure our work results in joy even when the process is difficult. We must enable our work to offer lessons that may be built upon and applied creatively during future opportunities. *"This is definitely not the life I signed up for!"* laughs Paula. *"I like where I am. I am happy and grateful. But I am very surprised! If you had told me when I finished college that this is where I would be living and working, I would have said, 'You're crazy!'"*

Wisdom and Wit about Education, Careers and Vocations

• "Never stop learning. The more I know, the more I realize what I don't know. This is humbling, and humility is good for the soul. I learned this from doing research as a tour guide, but it applies to the rest of my life as well. There is always more to learn, and as long as I keep learning, I will never feel bored."
• Read, read, read! Read fiction to learn about places, characters, and plots that differ from your own life. Read nonfiction to learn history, science, geography, and politics. Read bound books and electronic books and listen to audio books. Read print newspapers and magazines as well as online versions. Read cereal boxes if you have nothing else to read!"
• "Get a library card. It is your ticket to the world."
• "Read challenged and 'banned books.' Find out for yourself why people object to them and form your own opinions."
• "Read to children— every day."
• Do not read the news first thing in the morning. Reading and listening to uplifting books, spiritual texts, and self-help books is helpful. I'm not saying it's going to solve all your problems, but it does help to widen your perspective, enhance your self-awareness, and remind you of ways that you can improve in the areas that mean the most to you. In my case, these books have helped me gain self-confidence, become aware of the ways I sabotage myself, and have boosted my happiness and well-being."
• "Be part of a community with whom you share a common interest, whether it's singing in a choir, exercising with a team, being part of a meditation group or a book club or something else that connects you with people and learning."
• "Travel— in your neighborhood, in your state, across the United States, and throughout the world, as your resources allow. As Robert Frost suggested, 'take the road less traveled.' Walk. Spend time in nature. Observe people. Ask questions and listen to what people say. Learn the history. Eat a new food. Learn a new language— or at least a few phrases! Be grateful for what you experience and for coming home!"
• Learn something new or revisit something you studied as a child - take a line dancing class or a belly dancing class— who cares if you have two left feet! Sing in the shower or in a choir— who cares if you can't carry a tune! Take

up a new activity - walking, bird watching, yoga, collage, pottery— whatever! Who cares if you aren't talented?"

- "It surprises me how many women don't like eating in restaurants or taking trips by themselves. I wish more women felt comfortable enough to get in a bathing suit and swim in the ocean, even if they feel they are chubby. Attend a symphony all by yourself and soak it all in. Walk through a museum solo so that you can take time with what you see. You have to have enough self-love to take yourself out on a date!"

- "Find something you love to do every day. Most of us have to work to earn money to pay the bills, but that doesn't mean you can't do something that you feel passionate about. It probably won't be your first job. It may not be your second job. It may be your family or volunteer work. You will find your calling eventually."

- Do a personal audit of your values, temperament, and skills. What is important to you? Creativity? Structure? Witnessing others learn and grow? Helping others heal and become more independent? Are you independent and disciplined enough to work at home? Do you communicate and manage conflict well enough to be a supervisor? Are you visionary enough to be entrepreneurial? Do you enjoy meeting new people enough to be in sales, event planning, or tourism? You can acquire new skills, but you can't change your temperament, and you shouldn't compromise your values."

- Don't let work define you; instead, you should define your work. And if you don't like your defined role at work, it's you who has to go. Find something else! Life is too short to be miserable at work."

- "Anything work-related that gives you tremendous stress today will feel very small in one or two weeks. You will barely remember it in a few months."

- "Pick your battles. If you find a battle worth fighting, ask yourself, 'Is this a hill you are prepared to die on?' If the answer is 'no,' take some deep breaths and let the moment pass."

- "People say this all the time, but it is both true and important. Recognize people— their names and their jobs. Know and respect the people who clean your office, the people who serve meals in the cafeteria, your clerical staff, the people who manage finances and human relations, and the people who repair your technology (especially them!)"

Chapter Five

Faith

"Faith sees the invisible, believes the unbelievable, and receives the impossible."
- Corrie Ten Boom

Faith is a word we use frequently but seldom fully understand. One way to define faith is having complete trust and confidence in someone or something. Faith incorporates not only trust and confidence but also loyalty and commitment. Although it is frequently used and understood in the context of religion (as in faith in a God), it may also be understood and applied in a secular manner. Thus, a person may have faith in oneself, in a concept such as education or marriage, in a person such as one's spouse or partner, as well as in a personal religious or theological belief system such as Buddhism, Christianity, Judaism, Islam, Taoism, or another guiding belief system. Using this broad definition, faith is a core theme in the lives of all of the women I interviewed.

When a woman has faith, she is better equipped to use her trust and confidence to achieve her dreams and goals. When a woman has faith, she is able to rely on loyalty and commitment to take action and to remain persistent. The faith articulated by the women I interviewed is as diverse as the women and their experiences, but these attributes are evident in all of them.

Although faith is often thought of as being unwavering, in reality, these women relied heavily on questioning their faith to dream, to set goals, and to determine their actions. They also experienced times when their faith wavered or was badly shaken by the outcomes of their expectations or actions. This was true regardless of whether the faith they described was faith in themselves, faith in a concept, faith in a person, or faith in a religious or spiritual tradition. What is also remarkably evident is that faith has given these women resilience and the capacity to persist, overcome, and learn from difficult experiences.

Faith in Oneself

As children and adolescents, most of the women (and I) struggled with trusting ourselves. Now, as adults, we understand the value of trusting ourselves more fully— our bodies, our minds, our voices, our beliefs, our experiences, and our connections with family and community.

All of the women I interviewed expressed having faith in themselves now that they are adults. Nevertheless, for most of us, this has been a hard-won faith and, for many, only achieved after years of challenges. Nearly every woman— no matter how accomplished they appear on the outside— confessed to childhood and adolescent battles with low self-esteem, anxiety, shyness, depression, disordered eating, succumbing to peer pressure, and/or fearing they weren't attractive enough or intelligent enough to succeed.

As adults, most of us recognize the time we wasted on these battles. While some women do regret a few of their decisions, most women accept their decisions now with a mixture of embarrassment, humor, and resilience. Beth shakes her head and frowns as she reflects on the dissolution of her marriage, *"After my divorce, fear led me to relinquish my power. Why did I doubt the path that God had paved for me? As a wife and mother, I hesitated to step beyond my familiar roles. Regrettably, I wasted precious time at 58 years of age… still angry, disappointed, and still feeling hurt from my divorce."* Lydia concurs, grimacing with some embarrassment, *"Reading my journals [about dating and break-ups] makes me so angry with my younger self. I just want to go back and shake some sense into her. Or put my arm around her and say, 'You're fine. You're okay just the way you are. You don't need anybody to save you or complete you.' Ugh! It exhausts and embarrasses me just to think about those years."*

However, as Lydia concludes now, *"What surprises me most about where I am at this point is how happy I am! I feel like each decade, I have been happier than the one before. Several years ago, my husband told me I was the happiest person he knows. I was shocked but delighted. 'I've worked hard to be happy,' I told him."*

Likewise, Vicki is reflective about some of her choices that led to her incarceration: *"Prison isn't the right solution for everyone, but it changed me for the better. It helped me see suffering outside of me. It gave me a sense of how important it is to have honesty and integrity."* Beth concurs, *"Life's teachings have molded me into a multi-faceted woman— colorful, confident, and spiritually attuned. Triumphs and setbacks have propelled me forward, and I hope that my story ignites joy in others."* Effie summarizes her faith in herself with these words: *"I am an amalgamation of gratefulness and apathy, peace and conflict, hope and despair, success and failure, confidence and fear, inquisitiveness and neglect."*

Faith in oneself is a cornerstone for having faith in concepts. Kate remembers her self-doubts as a young woman: *"My fear was that others would find out about my medical condition and that it would influence my relationships with others. I also feared the impact it would have on my ability to marry and have a family of my own. That fear was allayed when I told [my future husband]. I learned to trust myself."* Another woman summarized, *"I had to learn to trust myself before I could trust marriage, friends, family, and church. Once I learned to trust myself, I was willing to reach out, take risks, and face adversity more confidently."*

Faith in Concepts
Education and Employment

Every woman I interviewed (including me) expressed faith in the concept of education and employment, that was instilled in us by our primary caregivers. As children, all of us pursued educational opportunities because we trusted that education was the correct path into adulthood. Whether our faith was in education as a pathway to marriage, a career, financial independence, or all of the above, was unimportant. We all believed that education would get us where we and/or our parents wanted us to go. We took action to commit to our goals. For example, Moonie illustrates her family's multi-generational faith in education: *"My family believed strongly in the benefits of education. My grandparents funded college educations for my parents, aunts, uncle, and siblings. I was the first of 23 who all graduated from college. I have continued the tradition, helping to fund education for my nieces and nephews."*

Whereas many parents had faith in education for their young daughters as a means to a career, successful marriage, and/or financial independence, as adults these women came to have faith in education for education's sake. "*Some days I feel overwhelmed by what I still want to learn, and I think to myself that I can't die yet because I still have so much to learn!*" jokes one woman. As adults, all of us have retained our faith in education as the vehicle to achieve our aspirations, but we have also come to have faith in education as a vehicle for self-discipline, as an outlet for creative passion, and for the sheer joy of learning.

Paula is a good example of someone who used her faith in education to creatively improvise jobs that would support her passion for travel. One day soon after graduating from college, on her way to a job she hated in Washington, DC, Paula serendipitously met a young woman at a bus stop who was about to enroll in a graduate program in travel and tourism. "*I wanted in! I needed this program!*" Paula exclaims, underscoring her lust for travel. She was accepted and recalls, "*The program was amazing!*" After graduating, Paula moved to Hawaii, where she secured a job teaching tourism education. "*I lived, breathed, and slept tourism for 11 years. For good measure, I got a part-time job with United Airlines and used their flight benefits whenever possible. I also learned to fly, earning my general aviation pilot's license.*" For Paula, her faith that education was a path to her travel aspiration enabled her to dream, set goals, and take action.

Similarly, Spice's faith in education was a way to embrace her passion for the cultural aspects of food. She pursued undergraduate and graduate degrees in nutrition and public health and then improvised her career path. Recognizing that her temperament might not be well suited to a job in the public sector, she embraced her entrepreneurial nature and established herself as a personal chef, focusing on healthy ethnic foods and culture. She credits her faith in education and in her cultural background. She summarizes this faith passionately and eloquently: "*Racism and xenophobia are prevalent in the food industry. For example, in 1968, an article in the New England Journal of Medicine falsely linked MSG to numbness, weakness, abdominal pain, and a rapid pulse. This became known as 'Chinese restaurant syndrome.' Ignorance and the white-dominated 'healthy* food' industry cause producers to set food standards from their perspective. These 'clean ingredients' are often narrowly defined, leaving out ingredients from other cultures with historical significance and health benefits. Food is not just feeding the stomach; it is feeding the soul."

Marriage and Family

Every woman I interviewed valued the concepts of marriage and family. Even those who have never married or who are divorced express their deep faith in the concepts. For some women, this faith is a by-product of their religious upbringing, their cultural heritage, and/or their parental role models. For others, their faith in marriage and family is deepened primarily by their faith in their chosen partners.

When Moonie married her wife, they had already been in a committed relationship for nearly 50 years. She credits her successful marriage to her lifelong faith in her partner, *"my amazing wife, who completes me."* She summarizes, *"Marriage is my major accomplishment. Everything else revolves around it."*

Joy and Beth both retained faith in the concept of marriage even though their marriages ended in divorce. Joy's breakup was very painful, but she summarizes, *"Our marriage was wonderful and surely appeared perfect to all who knew us, and yet it ended when I was faced with only one option. Walk away from the man who loved me, was the co-parent I needed for our children, and yet kept secret something that would destroy our marriage. I loved him, I still love him, but I could not support what he chose not to fix."* For both Joy and Beth, their Christian faith sustained them during their difficult divorces. Their faith also enabled them to learn from their experiences while also retaining their faith in the concept of marriage, a faith they model for their families and friends.

Beth elaborates, *"I told my pastor that I wanted to hurt [my ex-husband] as much as he had hurt me. He told me that forgiveness is what I should work on. Many months after my divorce, I still grappled with anger and self-esteem. My frustration with God grew. I questioned why God had allowed me this hardship. Reluctantly, I began attending divorce workshops. I listened to others' stories and learned from their experiences."* Over time, Beth felt that she was beginning to recover, and she shared her feelings proudly with her son: "*I want to help others as my spiritual response. I thought he would be supportive. His unexpected challenge was, 'How can you assist others when you still struggle?' Initially angry, I now consider this the truth. If this is my purpose, God will show me the way.*"

Joy understands and concurs with Beth. "*I continue to pray for him, [but] I no longer tell the story, not the one with anger. I learned that anger is debilitating and a huge block in our personal development. Anger takes over, and when you give in to it, you can't feel any joy or gratitude in life. Once I was able to forgive him, the heavy weight and darkness that anger hit me with was gone, gone, gone!*"

Not surprisingly, faith in marriage and family are important for those women who remain married or partnered. Lydia describes the gifts her husband brought to her life in opening her eyes to politics and current events and lists her children as their greatest accomplishment. Kate, who married her high school sweetheart and raised two sons with him, delights in the time they now spend with their adult sons and grandchildren. Vicki, who is not married, and Moonie, Paula, Spice, and I, who do not have children, all value our families and describe strong and warm relationships with nieces and nephews.

Similarly, Effie, who is widowed and does not have biological children of her own, delights in the relationships she has with her late husband's children, grandchildren, and sisters. Effie's faith evolved throughout her life. Growing up in a divorced family with no contact with her father, she relied on her Christian faith to guide her when she married. Loyalty and commitment became her beacons as she initially struggled to define her role as a wife and stepmother. Ultimately, these roles became an integral part of who she is today.

Spice, at age 26, is in a relationship but not married yet. "*We have to learn to take care of ourselves first!*" she jokes. Spice has faith in the concept of marriage and family that is strongly influenced by her Vietnamese culture: "*In my culture, family comes before all.*" Joy also recalls her childhood faith in family fondly: "*My grandparents came from Italy with only a few dollars in their pockets. We had many cultural practices, like dinner at Grandma's every Sunday. As a teenager, you didn't make any other plans and certainly not with a boyfriend!*" Kate agrees, "*Faith and devotion to family were paramount in my upbringing."*

Faith in Theological or Spiritual Belief Systems

Faith in a traditional religious system is a foundational aspect in the lives of many women. In some cases, religion was an important aspect of childhood— weekly or more frequent church attendance, parental leadership roles in church, religious education, church camps, and youth groups. In other cases, religion did not become important until adolescence and adulthood when we began strengthening our own values and voices. Some women retained the faith and practices of their childhoods, and others either found a new system that better met their values or abandoned theological faith entirely.

Effie, for example, attended the Methodist church throughout her Alabama childhood, including church camp during her teenage years. She graduated from Berry College, a non-denominational Christian-based college, which deeply informed her professional values and goals. She worked with The Upper Room, including ministry in Africa and prison ministry in Morganton. *"I found my husband in prison,"* she jokes. *"At age 53, I married the prison chaplain."*

Others, Lydia, for example, describe a more spiritual than traditional religious path. Her parents made an intentional decision not to provide a specific religious foundation. Lydia explains, *"My parents were not very religious. Although they both grew up going to the Methodist church, they decided not to have my sister and me baptized, telling us that they thought it was a personal decision better made on our own when we were adults."* Paula adds, *"We attended a Presbyterian church as children, but by the time we got to a certain age, my parents figured out that our moral compasses were set plus or minus one degree or so, and they didn't insist we attend anymore. They let me explore and question faith... they didn't mind us using our heads."*

Similarly, Dorothy comments, *"My Chinese parents were atheists— not religious at all."* Nevertheless, she attended a Catholic school for girls in Hong Kong, an experience that not only provided her with a quality education but also gave her a foundation in the Catholic faith. *"Catholicism has been a very important part of my life, even though I was not bap-*

tized until I was 20 years old. We were later married in the same church." As a busy professional, wife, and mother, she has improvised. "*We no longer attend church, but I pray in my own way much like when I was a child.*"

No matter their upbringing, in nearly every case, the women view their faith in something other than themselves as a source of deep personal understanding, a way of connecting with their inner selves, a source for their moral code, and a route for their spiritual direction and growth. Lydia describes her spiritual journey this way: "*The fact that my parents did not choose to baptize me opened the door for me to explore various spiritual paths on my own. In my childhood, I read parts of both the Old and New Testaments, I went to Methodist, Presbyterian, and Catholic services with friends. Later, I dated a Jewish man, went to a Seder, and learned more about that religion. With a tour group, I was introduced to the Muslim faith at the Islamic Center in Washington, DC.*" She continues, "*Over the years, I've read sacred texts from many different religions but ended up gravitating toward Buddhism. I started meditating daily. Meditation changed my life. It was a true awakening for me!*"

One summer, when Lydia had been waking up depressed for several months, she decided that she would go to a local bookstore "*with the thought that the Universe would point me to what I needed to pull myself out of my misery.*" She came across a translation of the Tao Te Ching that changed her life. "*Twelve years later, I am still reading the Tao, usually one verse a day. At this point, I have read over 30 renditions of the text, many of them more than once, and each reading has brought me a greater depth of understanding.*" She concludes, "*I am eternally grateful to my parents for trusting me to find my own spiritual path. I am so happy that I listened to the Universe the day of that desperate visit to the bookstore. It ended up being a life-changing event for me.*"

Effie describes her spiritual journey this way: "*My faith has gone through lots of transformations, but it has become deeper with age, experiences, and difficulties. [I] truly believe God has breathed life into each of us. Although I will be the first to admit that I often fall short, my desire is to recognize God within every person and to know more deeply the God who is exquisitely personal in presence and grace for each of us and for our hurting world.*"

Beth's Christian faith was badly shaken by the dissolution of her marriage. *"After my divorce, I was angry and uncertain."* She prayed for guidance about the next leg of her journey, and she believes that she received three firm nudges to apply to the Peace Corps, *"something I never planned, never wanted to do."* There were many obstacles— her anger and her age, as well as the cultural differences between her life and health care career in the United States and the expectations and realities of life and work in Zambia, Africa. Nevertheless, her faith sustained her during the application and training process.

Once in Africa, Beth's faith was initially shaky. She was still angry and resentful. She smiles now, remembering *"praying to be injured, to be sent home"* during her early months in the Peace Corps, and only later recognizing the tremendous personal impact her time in Zambia had on her faith. Beth describes a pivotal moment that occurred one day in Africa as she sat outdoors by herself struggling with her anger and doubts. *"To my left, an ant fought to escape her tangled prison of leaves, dirt, and sticks. Her struggle mirrored mine…when she stilled, I mourned her demise, sensing my own surrender. But then, the debris fell away, and she emerged— alive and unburdened! I realized that, within me, there bloomed untapped abilities, transcending imagined boundaries. The words 'I can' replaced my doubt."*

I was not raised in a family with a religious foundation. I was baptized as a young adult after exploring the Episcopal Church. Today, I consider myself to be an unapologetic but poorly educated Episcopalian. Unapologetic because I feel grounded in the traditions and teachings of the Episcopal church and poorly educated because my religious education has been largely self-directed. My faith is my foundation for what I value and how I spend my time and other resources, but, like many of the women I interviewed, my religious faith has been a journey of improvisation that continues today.

Lydia, Beth, Effie, Joy, Vicki, and I all rely on our faith in a religious or spiritual tradition to help us improvise a way forward when faced with intermittent depression, illness, divorce, death of a spouse, and other losses. Our faith enables us to trust ourselves and to trust God or the Universe outside of ourselves. Finally, our faith enables us to take action and to persist once our path forward becomes clearer.

Wisdom and Wit About Faith

- "Be yourself. Trust yourself. Know your worth."
- If you don't believe in yourself, if you don't trust yourself, nothing else really matters. To be a friend, to be a partner or spouse, to pursue a vocation, to be a parent, you must first believe in yourself."
- Spend some time defining what is important to you— your values. Commit them to memory and let them be your guidepost for every decision you make, every word you speak, and every action you take. Your values will deepen as you age, but they will not change unless you change them. Your response to everything that happens to you should reflect your values. If not, you either need to change your responses or change your values. You choose."
- As women, and especially as women of color, we don't give ourselves enough self-compassion and enough grace and tenderness. Ask for what you need. Set boundaries. Allow yourself to be your own fierce self."
- "Faith and depression are not mutually exclusive. Recognize this in yourself and in others."
- "From childhood to adulthood, my life has been a winding journey— a series of unexpected twists and turns. God's voice has always encouraged me to persevere and achieve my long-held dreams. As an older adult, joy radiates from my core. Now my life's mission is to receive and share this unspeakable joy. No external force can steal it; I guard it fiercely."
- While I do not practice the faith of my parents, learning and practicing the tenets of faith about love, hope, and forgiveness are important in how I have responded to the challenges and successes I have experienced."
- Let things happen organically; don't push for things to happen. Look for signs that you are on the right path. The right path is lit up like an airport runway with few, if any, obstacles. When you push for things that aren't meant to be, obstacles present themselves, and you must question whether you are on the right path and if it is worth the fight to make it your path."
- "Recognize that God is within each person you will encounter. Be kind."
- "Embark upon your own journey of faith. Savor every foolish misstep as well as every accomplishment. It should be a lifelong journey of trust, hope, action, persistence, and gratitude."

Chapter Six

Marriage, Partnerships, and Children
"*I have learned not to worry about love; but to honor it with all my heart.*"
- Alice Walker

Marriage and other long-term partnerships play an important role in the lives of nearly all the women I interviewed. Some women married relatively young, while other women married later in life. Some women remain married today while others found their marriages ended by divorce or death. Two women have never been married, but one is in a long-term relationship with her partner. Some women chose to raise children, some women inherited them through marriage, some women chose not to have children, and one young woman, Spice, thinking optimistically about her future, exclaims, "*I am still not ready to take care of myself— much less children!*"

Marriage and the Partnerships we Create

Moonie and her partner have been together since college, for nearly 50 years, and they have been married since gay marriage became legal in their home state in 2013. "*Marriage is my greatest accomplishment. My wife is the most ethical and caring human being I have ever met. We have a perfect rhythm. We can be quiet together, and we can be boisterous together.*" Moonie credits her family's influence and acceptance— parents, grandmother, and siblings— for her confidence living as a lesbian and with her successful long-term marriage.

Effie married late in life (at age 53) and did not raise children of her own. As a result, when she met and married her husband and inherited his children and grandchildren, she had to improvise. Crafting the role of wife, stepmother, and step-grandmother from her childhood experiences, and her husband and his family's experiences and expectations was a significant challenge. *"It has been tough work, but having his family in my life continues to be one of my greatest joys."*

Joy's marriage and children shaped her life in life-altering ways, both professionally and personally. She married her husband, *"the man of her dreams,"* when she was 23. *"He was fun, easygoing, handsome, and best of all, he wanted lots of children too!"* Together, they raised five children, completed graduate degrees, and were active members of their community and their children's athletic lives.

As their children became teenagers, they combined their considerable professional talents to establish an executive leadership training and coaching business. They garnered clients all over the United States, the United Kingdom, Canada, and Africa. She noted, *"We were stars and treated as such. Life was good. Everything was as I had dreamed, almost too good to be true. And then, one night, I received a phone call that led me to understand that I had been living totally in a dream world; my life was not at all as it seemed."*

This phone call began a multi-year trajectory that ended both her marriage and her business partnership with her husband. Her husband called her from a business trip to say that he was going to be arrested for making *"a sexually explicit phone call to a random telephone number."* The woman he called contacted the police, and the phone call was traced to her husband's hotel room. Joy was in shock, *"I didn't understand, this was not at all like the man I married, who loved me and was raising a family with me. I became aware of this horrible feeling in my stomach…that horrible 'I think I am going to vomit' feeling that was to become how I would feel every day for the next seven years."*

Over the next few months, as Joy learned more details about her husband's activities, it became clear how deep and long-term his betrayals had been and how out of control his sexual addiction was. It took several years for Joy to fully accept this, but eventually, and with full support of her adult children, she and her husband quietly divorced. She reflects on the sadness she felt at the end of her marriage: *"I told him if he would consent to weekly counseling…I would stay in the marriage. He said he did not need therapy; he could take care of the problem. To this day, I am shocked by his response that could have kept us together and kept him on a path…to control his addiction."*

Children

The women who raised children count their children's success as adults as one of their greatest accomplishments. With grown children and, in some cases, grandchildren, Lydia, Joy, and Kate are proud of their adult children. Lydia is unapologetic: *"At the risk of sounding overly momish, I have to admit that raising two wonderful human beings is my proudest accomplishment."* Joy agrees, *"One of my proudest accomplishments is the raising…of my five children. Each of my children is known in the business world for their ability to lead, to recognize others for their accomplishments, to root for others, and to serve others by giving back. I am continually surprised at my children's successes and how much they include me in their business and social lives."*

Beatrice describes her role in modeling advocacy skills for her teenage son, and her pride in her young son's self-advocacy skills. *"[My son] walked away from his 7th grade award ceremony with two awards. Last year, he had multiple suspensions, lunch detentions, and [in-school suspensions], and spent quite some time getting to know the school principal! Academically, he was near failing. He was the kid labeled as 'bad' and they didn't know how to support him…I shared countless research articles with the school and pushed and pushed. This year, at the beginning of school, he went into his [Individualized Education Program] meeting and took charge. He told them what works for him and what doesn't. They listened. And he succeeded. I'm so proud of this dude for so many reasons!"*

The women who chose not to have children have no regrets about the decision, but they do value their relationships with other family members and friends as significant components of their adult lives. One woman notes, *"I chose not to have children and I have never regretted the decision. Being childless has given me the independence I want, and it has also given me an opportunity to develop close relationships with my friends' children and with my nieces and nephews.* Paula advises, *"I didn't have children and I have zero regrets. Please don't feel compelled to have children just to conform to societal norms."* As for me, my voluntary childlessness led to my career in education and advocacy. I know I made a difference in the lives of many children, and I am grateful for this.

Wisdom and Wit About Marriage, Partnerships, and Children

- *Marriage is difficult. Really difficult. You both have to commit to the long game. Even so, all marriages end— either in divorce or death. Learn to forgive; don't waste time on anger."*
- *Before and during the early years of marriage, share your expectations about marriage with your spouse or partner. It took me many years and a lot of misunderstandings to realize that my husband couldn't read my mind!"*
- "It's unwise to expect your partner to fulfill your every need. Cultivate friendships and interests outside of your marriage."
- "Figure out how to live on your own without men. I don't say this because I am a lesbian. Just learn how to be independent and be able to rely on yourself. This will make you a better partner and friend."
- *Nurture your friendships. In my younger and desperate dating days, I often neglected my friends since I was so busy focusing on the 'man of the moment.' I am so grateful that my friends stuck by me and were there for me when these relationships ended."*
- *Sustain your long-time friends and keep making new friends. Take inventory of those friends who are your cheerleaders, those who are your warriors, those who are your counselors, and those who you can always depend on whether it is to join you for a glass of wine, provide a shoulder to cry on, walk the dog, or just listen without advising."*
- " Don't say 'No!' to a toddler unless they are doing something dangerous. There are other ways to say it that won't set off a tantrum. For example, 'Maybe we can do that later, but right now, we're going to do this instead.'"
- "One of my great accomplishments, even though I did not have children, is having strong relationships with my younger family members. I feel like I played a role in their accomplishments. I am humbled and honored that they want to spend so much time with me."
- "My husband and I had a long-distance relationship for more than 8 years. My younger self would never have had the self-confidence to live on my own. I was surprised by how much I enjoyed living alone and I think it enhanced our relationship. He taught me a lot about independence and self-sufficiency.

Chapter Seven

Losses, Disappointments, and Resilience

"You gain strength, courage, and confidence by every experience in which you really stop to look fear in the face. You are able to say to yourself, 'I lived through this horror. I can take the next thing that comes along.' You must do the thing you think you cannot do."
– Eleanor Roosevelt

By the time most women reach adulthood and certainly by middle-age, it would be impossible to imagine a life without the experience of several losses and disappointments. Significant losses might include the death of parents, siblings, close friends, and/or spouses. They might include the loss of a career, the loss of a marriage or other severed relationships, or the loss of one's health or physical abilities. Disappointments might include the realization that a desired career goal won't be met, the realization that giving birth to a child is no longer possible, the acknowledgement that one's adult children have made unexpected choices, or the realization that writing a bestselling book is not likely to happen.

Some losses and disappointments that feel overwhelming to us may appear small and insignificant to others - the death of a beloved pet or the loss of a family heirloom ring, for example. Other losses and disappointments may be devastating to us as well as to others - the diagnosis of a disability in oneself or a child, the death of a sibling, or the betrayal and infidelity of a long-time partner. However, for several women I interviewed, over time, initially devastating losses and disappointments became *"life-altering calls to action"* for the women experiencing them.

Grief

Grief is a natural response to loss and disappointment. It doesn't just apply to loss of life; I think we can (and arguably should) grieve over any significant loss or disappointment. We can grieve because we feel like our dreams have been shattered, or because our faith has been shaken to its core. As we grieve, we remember when things were different, when we believed life was better than it is now. Grief can unleash a lot of different emotions - anguish, guilt, depression, anger, fear, and shame. Lydia agrees: "Many changes in my life came about because of what I would have called 'disasters' at the time they occurred. They forced me to learn strategies to deal with the disappointment and depression that arose because of them. Looking back, I believe they actually ended up leading to progress and making me happy."

For some, grief such as the earth-shattering blow of a spouse's infidelity or the birth of a child with a disability can be life-altering. Joy reminisces about the tremendous infidelity and betrayal in her marriage: "I have had some difficult challenges and while I didn't like them or choose them, I got through them, and frankly I am in a better, stronger, more grounded place as a result of them." Kate recalls the diagnosis of her son with Down syndrome: "My initial feelings were fear, uncertainty, anger, and guilt." She remembers feeling deep sadness when she learned of her son's diagnosis, thinking, "All the dreams and hopes I had for my child were gone. I was also angry and afraid because our lives were going to be very difficult dealing with the challenges and uncertainties of having a child with his diagnosis."

Moonie's mother was an excellent swimmer, but when her little sister was nine years old, the family experienced a tragic loss; her mother died in a drowning accident. "I had just graduated from college and was working as a lifeguard. My mother was drinking and swimming late at night and hit her head and died" in the nearby lake where the family had spent weekends and summers for many years. "My dad was broken. I had just finished college. I had three brothers and sisters still in college and my nine-year old sister needed care." Even while grieving, Moonie improvised. She researched universities that were offering assistantships and enrolled in graduate school part-time so that she could work, go to school, and help her grandmother raise her youngest sister.

Beatrice recalls vividly the most traumatic event in her life, the death of her older sister that occurred when she was in middle school. "*That morning my sister left for school in her red Nissan. It was a rainy Wednesday and I was getting ready for middle school. Before my sister left, I asked her if I could wear her navy polo shirt. I never thought that would be the last conversation I would have with my sister.* [When I heard that she had died in a car accident]... *I was devastated. I fell to the floor and started throwing up. Her friend was screaming and everything around me just became numb. I don't remember much after that except my dad getting there and me giving him a big hug as we both cried. Our family was shattered by the loss of my sister.*"

I think that each of these women would agree that while their experiences were life-altering and certainly not welcome, ultimately the experience and the grief that followed made them both stronger and more compassionate women today.

Anger

Beth and Joy both felt tremendous anger toward their spouses when they betrayed their faith in marriage and family. Beth expresses her anger strongly, "*His dismissal of 37 years? I was so very angry. I wanted revenge!*" She wondered, "*Would God forgive me for thinking this way? This was my lifelong dream— to be married to this man all my life and to be a mother.*" Joy understands: "*At first, I was so angry that* [my husband] *messed up our lives that I didn't see what I needed to do to find my way. In my anger, I spent way too much time talking about what he did, how hurt we all were. Angry thoughts took up way too much of my days.* Eventually, Joy learned "*that anger is debilitating and a huge block in our personal development. Anger takes over, and when you give in to it, you can hardly feel any joy or gratefulness.*"

Forgiveness

As Joy adjusted to her life as a single woman and began improvising her new path in life, she learned that her ex-husband had been diagnosed with Parkinson's disease and was struggling both physically and financially. She realized that she had wasted too much time on anger and that at her core, she was a compassionate and forgiving woman. So, Joy called him and offered him *"a deal that was difficult for him to pass up. I would send him a plane ticket to Florida where I was living. He couldn't live with me, but I would find a place nearby for him and pay the rent for the rest of his life. 'What's the catch?' he asked. You have to come with me to a neurologist and if necessary, commit to regular visits with the doctor. I will go with you to all your appointments. I will oversee your care, and if, in time, you need a different level of care, I will make sure that you have it. He didn't have much of a choice, and so he readily agreed."*

Next, Joy summoned the courage to tell their adult children about her plan. *"I expected them to say that I was nuts or ask what I was thinking. However, there was dead silence. Finally, the youngest of my sons said, 'Wow, mom, that's what you have talked about all our lives…taking care of each other…forgiving…family takes care of family.'* Joy was relieved, but also proud of the values she had modeled for her children. She continues, *"So here is the learning point in all of this. I knew I had finally, after seven long painful years, let go of the anger. I had forgiven him."*

Today, Joy advises, *"If you have anger, please ask for help. Figure out how to put it away, get ahead of it, and take charge of your journey. Don't waste all your good energy, use it to improve your life. Learn from it! We all have challenges and while we don't like it when they are happening to us, once we get through them, we are stronger, better, and less afraid of another challenge we may face down the line."*

Shortly after her son's birth, Kate recalls listening to a taped lecture about the impact the birth of a child with a disability has on parents. *"It validated much of what I had been feeling in regards to grief and anger. I came to realize that these were typical feelings, which helped me to stop feeling guilty about not feeling the joy one expects to feel upon the birth of a child. He said the loss one experiences is about the future you envision, and one can move beyond that loss by replacing that imagined future with a different vision for the child… to 'dream new dreams.'"*

Today, Kate reflects on family life with her son with Down syndrome: *"I came to realize that my initial feelings were typical…help from others enabled me to envision a life for [my son], to have expectations that I don't think that I would have had without these opportunities and folks sharing their knowledge, experiences, and encouragement. I came to realize that* he would have his own learning style, and he would learn those things that were of interest to him. I came to realize that he has an innate kindness about him and is almost always cheerful, which endears him to others. While he enjoys routine in his life, he has also proven to be very adaptable when change is required. I think these are rare qualities in all of us as we age."* Today, her son works in a cat coffee shop and enjoys rich relationships with family and community members.

Resilience

Resilience is the ability to *"bounce back"* from adversity, to successfully incorporate the guilt, grief, anger, sadness, disappointment and other feelings we may have in order to adapt and persist. Resilience is not a characteristic that people are born with or not; it is something we build over time with practice.

As painful as it seemed at the time, the women who shared stories of loss and disappointment eventually moved on from their grief, anger, and other feelings. That is not to say that they *"got over"* their experiences, or that they wouldn't have preferred to forgo their experiences entirely. They were definitely changed by the experiences, and at first, they were unsure how or even if they could move forward.

They took time to grieve, feel anger, and then they took time to creatively improvise their next steps. They began to reflect, plan, and integrate what they learned into their path forward. For some, like Beatrice and Kate, their loss and disappointment informed their vocations and work. For others, like Joy and Beth, their losses and disappointment required time and reflection to overcome their initial feelings and forgive. For others, like Lydia, her losses and disappointments made her a more grateful woman.

Wisdom and Wit About Losses, Disappointment, and Resilience

- *"Food, and especially dessert, helps heal a lot of the pain caused by grief. So, eat all the cake offered to you!"*
- *I believe having grace as a value influences how we treat others and our-*

selves, especially when disappointed. We all make mistakes. Judging or condemning mistakes humiliates a person and can result in guilt that is detrimental to relationships and mental well-being. Offering grace to others and ourselves during times of disappointment provides hope for improvement and better things to come."

• Each day is just one day. Change is inevitable and offers opportunities for growth."

• Each of us is viewing the world through the lens of our own experiences. Very few people can polish their 'inner mirror' so it flawlessly reflects reality as it truly is, without the filter of their own biases, expectations and opinions."

• "Smile at other people. Smiling is infectious. It literally tricks your brain into thinking you are feeling happy. I like to call a smile the best make-up."

• Face your fears. Practice self-care and self-compassion. Meditate. Cultivate forgiveness."

Chapter Eight

Summary

"I'm not interested in being perfect when I'm older. I'm interested in having a narrative. It's the narrative that's really the most beautiful thing about being a woman."
- Jodie Foster

When I began the process of interviewing women for this book, I tried hard not to predict the themes that might emerge. I wanted their stories to emerge without any preconceived direction or boundaries. I wanted their stories to be spontaneous and uninhibited. I believe that what has emerged is a rich narrative about women who are unafraid to be honest, vulnerable, spontaneous, angry, forgiving, and joyful. That is, women who aren't afraid to be improvisational.

As I noted in Chapter One, as an introvert, I wrestled with whether to include my own story, and after considerable thought, I decided to take a risk and add my own voice. I hope I have been half as courageous and thoughtful as the 11 women I interviewed.

Once I completed the interviews and wrote my own responses, I read and re-read the written responses, and I listened and re-listened to the interviews. I made marginalia and I color-coded. I woke up more than a few nights at 3 AM with an *"aha"* thought and ran to my computer to double-check a quote or make a note about something that I wanted to think about more fully during daylight hours. Eventually, I coded everyone's stories in order to capture shared themes.

As a retired researcher, I feel compelled to offer a few words of caution here. Because this is a qualitative narrative, the themes may or may not generalize to other women, even to those of similar demographics and with similar experiences. That is, each woman's story is her own. She does not represent every woman of color, every lesbian, every woman who grew up in a Christian household, every woman who emigrated to the United States, every middle-aged woman, and so forth. It is equally true that my reflections throughout this book, and in this concluding chapter, are my own. You, as a reader, may (and should) consider your own reflections about what you have learned after reading each woman's words and lived experiences.

What Have I Learned From Writing This Book?

First, and most importantly, I have learned that women are more courageous than we give ourselves credit for being. The courage to be vulnerable, to be honest, to share, to create, to trust, to forgive, and to laugh at ourselves is evident in every woman's story. Courage requires trust in ourselves and in others. It requires time to emerge, and it requires relationships to thrive.

Courageous women must be improvisational. We might begin with models and maps from our childhoods, but by adulthood, we realize that there is no road map to follow. Instead, we must take tentative, small steps. Sometimes, we must leap forward even when we fear that there may be insurmountable obstacles or dangerous detours ahead of us. As several women concluded, once they trusted themselves to consider options and take action, the roadblocks and disappointments that seemed so overwhelming melted away. "*Expect anything worthwhile to take a long time and to be hard work*, summarizes one woman, "*be courageous and don't expect life to turn out the way you imagined or planned.*"

Second, I have learned that having both faith and a purpose in life can buffer the impact of life's stressors and make us resilient. As I finalize this book at the beginning of 2025, I and many women I talk to are questioning our faith and our purpose. *Do we still have faith in America and in Democracy? Do we still have faith in ourselves? What is our purpose during what feels like a chaotic time to so many of us?* Although we may feel insecure, we may doubt ourselves, and we may doubt our faith in whatever we believe, we are resilient. We may have absolutely no idea how to move forward— or even if we can. But over time, we will begin to trust ourselves again, we will find our voices, we will share our stories with others, and we will take action. In short, we will improvise our next steps. We will remember that we are indeed resilient.

Third, forgive, forgive, forgive. And keep forgiving. Our relationships are like sunny days that startle us with sudden and unexpected thunderstorms. We must shake off the raindrops and transform our anger, shame, disappointment, sorrow, jealousy— whatever we are feeling— into strength, compassion, and love. When we forgive, others bear witness to our model, and others, too, learn to forgive.

Forgiveness is extraordinarily difficult. (I certainly have not mastered the skill yet!) Forgiveness requires improvisation. When you don't know how to forgive, how to move past your grief, pain, and anger, you must imagine how the future will look differently. It will change you, but you must not let it define you. You must take one small step forward, leaving the experience and emotions behind you. And then take one more step, and another, and another. If you don't forgive, you will remain mired in the morass of grief, anger, and despair.

Fourth, I have learned that wisdom is accepting that hope and despair must live side-by-side within all of us. We cannot fully live without both hope and despair, without both love and loss, or without both joy and sorrow. We cannot feel love without being open to disappointment and loss. We cannot appreciate joy without being open to grief and sorrow. I have learned also that wit is the ability to share one's wisdom with others with joy and humor. Sharing wit is contagious; it results in smiles and playfulness with others. Sharing wit is the epitome of improvisational living.

Fifth, I have learned the importance of community. Sharing our experiences with family, friends, neighbors, colleagues, church and club members, etc., builds our courage, our faith, our purpose, and our wisdom. We cannot fully live without putting ourselves out there. We cannot fully live without sharing with each other. Thus, throughout our lives, improvisation will play an important role in shaping us as wives, partners, mothers, stepmothers, grandmothers, aunts, friends, entrepreneurs, employees, advocates, volunteers, and/or other contributors to our communities.

And finally, I have learned not only to resist cynicism, but to actively fight it with gratitude. Cynicism is lazy, lonely, and destructive. Gratitude is active, engaged, and affirming. Several women described how gratitude practices, including prayer and meditation, help them during difficult times. I practice gratitude every day in my silent prayers, and in my written journal, I remind myself daily of *"one good thing."*

Lessons of Improvisational Women

As a result of being improvisational, our life stories are not written solely by us. They are written by all the people who enter and exit our lives, by all the loves and losses we experience, by all the times we try and succeed, and by all the times we try and fail. No one can fully tell us how to improvise our lives— not our parents, teachers, friends, church leaders, or partners. Of course, we must listen and learn from them, but in the end, we must creatively improvise our very own individual and imperfect lives. Along the way, we edit the stories we tell ourselves and we edit the stories others tell us. The result is a rich musical score of both structure and improvisation that we perform. We can only hope that in the end, we smile and say to ourselves, *"It was truly worth improvising that music!"*

The Interview Questions

Some readers may find it interesting to interview their loved ones— friends, family, and partners— in order to learn more about their lived experiences. Others may find it informative to respond to the questions themselves. These are the four questions I used with the women I interviewed for this book. Feel free to use them, revise them, or discard them and write your own!

1. **Tell me about your childhood and teenage years.**
    - Where were you born and raised?
    - Who were the important people during your childhood and teenage years?
    - What cultural, religious, or family expectations impacted your childhood and teenage years?
    - What challenges did you face? What opportunities came your way?
    - What were your fears? What were your hopes and dreams?

2. **Tell me about your adult years.**
    - What education, work, relationship, family, health, volunteer, travel, and/or other experiences have shaped your adult years?
    - How have your childhood and teenage experiences carried you through adulthood?
    - What challenges have you faced? What opportunities have come your way?
    - What have been your fears? What have been your hopes and dreams?

3. **Thinking back on your life so far...**
    - What has been your proudest accomplishment? What did you learn about yourself as you accomplished this?
    - What and/or who do you value most in your everyday life? How do these values shape the way you spend your time?
    - What surprises you most about where you are at this point in your life?
    - What do you still fear? What hopes and dreams do you still have?

4. **Looking back at what you have shared so far, what wisdom and wit have you acquired that you think is important for other women to know?**
    - What makes you "you"? Is there a part of your life story that makes you the wise woman you are today? A story that others might benefit from?
    - Is there an opportunity or challenge that you wish more women could experience?
    - Do you have a personal characteristic or value that you wish more women would embrace? For example, humor, gratitude, resilience, family, faith, etc.

Book Club Discussion Questions

1. Take a minute to look at the artwork on the cover of this book. What do you think the women looking at the art see? What do you see?

2. Which woman's story most resonated with you? Which woman's story least resonated with you? Why?

3. Do you think there are universal themes in women's lives regardless of their cultural, racial, ethnic, disability, or other defining characteristics? If so, what are they? If not, why?

4. What childhood experiences have impacted who you are today? How have they done so?

5. What role have educational expectations and experiences played in your life?

6. Do you have a vocation? If so, what is it? How does it inform who you are?

7. Describe your job history and career path. What successes and obstacles have you encountered along the way?

8. How do you define faith? Has faith in something or someone been important in your life?

9. What role have marriage, partnerships, and children played in your life?

10. How have loss and disappointments impacted who you are today?

Other Suggested Activities

1. Gather poster board, magazines, scissors, color markers, and glue and create your own vision board. You don't have to do this as a New Year's project. It might be for your birthday, for a new job or relationship, or just because it is a rainy, cold Monday!

2. Start a "Women Sharing Wisdom" group in your community or seek out an existing group. (Refer to Dr. Beth Firestein's "A Facilitator's Guide" in the resource list at the end of this book.)

3. Think about one or more of the creative and improvisational women in your life. Share with her why her life inspires you. Ask her to share her wisdom and wit with you.

Suggested Resources for Those Interested in Learning More

Bateson, M. C. (1989). *Composing a Life.* New York: Atlantic Monthly Press.

Bateson, M.C. (2010). *Composing a Further Life. The Age of Active Wisdom*. New York: Penguin Random House.

Firestein, B. (2022). *Women Sharing Wisdom. A Facilitator's Guide to Starting a Wise Women Group*. Author.

Lewis, L. (Edited). (2023). *Women who Changed the World: Stories From the Fight for Social Justice*. San Francisco: City Lights Books.

Moore, C. (2023). *The Lives of Extraordinary Women: The Untold Stories of Women who Changed the Course of History*. Author.

Acknowledgments

I have been blessed throughout my life to have had dozens of people who have contributed to my vision for this book: teachers who taught me to love reading and writing, students who trusted me to critique their writing, and colleagues who co-wrote with me. There is no way to thank them all, but I hope every reader will take a moment to quietly thank the educators in their own lives.

My heartfelt gratitude goes to the women who allowed me to interview them. I am truly overwhelmed by your trust in telling me your stories and your belief that I could pull this project together. There are no words to thank you enough!

There are dozens of other women whom I wish I could have included in this book. Too many names to mention here, but I suspect that you know who you are. Your friendships have brought laughter, tears, regrets, love, loss, and wisdom. You all have a place in my heart and in this book. Thank you for your friendship.

Patty Thompson with Redhawk Publications was both a cheerleader and a coach. Thank you for every piece of sage advice you shared with me.

Thank you to my mother who at age 93 still reads 5-7 books a week. Thank you to my husband who stayed out of my way while I wrote this book and never questioned my middle of the night writing sessions. And lastly, thank you to all the four-legged creatures in my life who remind me to live in the moment.

About The Cover Artist

The cover art was created by North Carolina artist, Missy Cleveland, a self-taught interpretative painter whose vibrant journey through the world of art has spanned more than 25 years. To learn more about Missy and her creations, visit her on Instagram: @_missycleveland_

About The Author

After earning degrees in special education and urban services from the University of Virginia and Virginia Commonwealth University, Jane spent 40 years as a high school special education teacher and advocate for adolescents and adults with disabilities and their families. She has lived and worked in Virginia, New York, Louisiana, North Carolina, and South Carolina.

Now retired, Jane lives in Hickory, North Carolina, with her husband and a menagerie of cats and dogs. She advocates for her 93-year-old mother, serves on her local school board, does volunteer work, reads voraciously, dabbles in vegetarian cooking, and creates community connections (and mischief) wherever she can.

While working, Jane authored dozens of written materials and online training modules on special education, leadership, and team building. This is her first "outside-the-box" post-retirement book.

Visit her Facebook page at: https://tinyurl.com/JaneEversonFacebook
E-mail her at: jmeverson@charter.net

www.ingramcontent.com/pod-product-compliance
Lightning Source LLC
Chambersburg PA
CBHW020948090426
42736CB00010B/1313